# Sunset
# Potluck
## COOK BOOK

*By the Editors of Sunset Books and Sunset Magazine*

*Lane Publishing Co.* ■ *Menlo Park, California*

Research & Text
**Cynthia Scheer**

Contributing Editor
**Susan Warton**

Coordinating Editor
**Linda J. Selden**

Design
**Joe di Chiarro**

Illustrations
**Susan Jaekel**

Photography
**Tom Wyatt**

Photo Stylist
**JoAnn Masaoka**

**Cover:** Taking potluck from the recipes in this cook book can produce a marvelous menu (clockwise from top): Spinach Salad with Basil Dressing (page 24), Sweet & Sour Baked Beans (page 37), and Amaretto Cheesecake (page 89), along with barbecued chicken and freshly baked corn muffins. Design by Sandra Popovich. Photography by Tom Wyatt. Photo styling by JoAnn Masaoka. Food styling by Elizabeth Friedman.

---

### About the Recipes

All of the recipes in this book were tested and developed in the *Sunset* test kitchens.

*Home Economics Editor, Sunset Magazine*
*Jerry Anne Di Vecchio*

---

## The More, the Merrier

Too many cooks may cause problems with soup, but with a potluck, the more who get involved, the merrier. That's why potlucks are so much fun—everyone gets into the act. The result? An abundance of good things to eat, from the first crudité to the last slice of cheesecake.

To join in the merrymaking, we've produced a potluck of our own. We invite you to sample the myriad recipes in this book for your next big event. Whether you choose a traditional favorite or something intriguingly new, you'll find many marvelous dishes that you can present with pride. Look through the menu suggestions, too. All of the recipes were developed for maximum ease of transport to the potluck site. Many include convenient make-ahead steps in their preparation. We hope that all will contribute to your potluck pleasure.

We wish to thank The Best of All Worlds for its generosity in sharing props for use in our photographs. Additionally, we thank Fran Feldman for her fine copyediting of our manuscript.

For our recipes, we provide a nutritional analysis (please see page 5) prepared by Hill Nutrition Associates, Inc., of New York.

Editor, Sunset Books: Elizabeth L. Hogan

Second printing December 1989

# Contents

*Potluck Planning & Menus 4*

*Appetizers 15*

*Salads & Vegetables 23*

*Fish & Shellfish 42*

*Poultry 55*

*Meats 71*

*Desserts 87*

*Index 95*

*Crowning swirls of spaghetti, Spicy Mediterranean Meatballs is just one of several sauces on the Pasta Party menu (page 12).*

## Special Features

*Breads for Non-bakers 29*

*Poach Now, Bake Later Fish 52*

*Holiday Turkey Dinner 60*

*Lasagne for a Crowd 76*

*Harvest Soup Party 84*

# Potluck Planning & Menus

From a simple brown bag picnic to a banquet for dozens of guests, the best meals are social occasions. Potlucks celebrate the social meal in a uniquely appetizing way.

At one time, "taking potluck" literally meant taking the luck of the day's pot. But today, the phrase promises much more than making do with whatever is on hand. Potlucks have become a popular form of carefree and casual entertaining.

## A group effort

Getting actively involved is what potluck dining is all about. From the host's point of view, it obviously helps when guests contribute to the dinner, especially when there's a large crowd. Guests, too, appreciate the chance to participate by bringing a favorite specialty. And everyone loves the tantalizing smorgasbord that results.

How many participants do you need for a potluck? One party might include just two or three couples, sharing their newest culinary triumphs. Or the guest list may span two or three family generations, gathering to celebrate a first birthday or a 50th wedding anniversary. Potlucks can even take in an entire club membership or suburban neighborhood.

Regardless of their numbers, all participants tend to agree on the ground rules: they want to have a great meal and a great time, while sharing a dish of which they can feel proud.

## Getting organized

Pooling the work involved in staging a large dinner has several practical advantages for the host. It saves cooking time, as well as part of the cost of entertaining. Often, it minimizes the cleanup afterward.

To organize all this help, first take a head count. Next, plan the meal—loosely or in detail. One popular method is to assign by menu categories (appetizers, salads, main dishes, side dishes, and desserts), leaving actual recipe choices up to the cooks. Or you may prefer to make specific assignments, even providing recipes if needed. Noncooked contributions can range from bakery bread to wine or paper plates.

When a potluck is held at home, it's often customary for the host family to provide the main course. Consider a roast, ham, or turkey—or, in fair weather, barbecued meat or poultry. Ask guests to round out the menu.

Keep in mind that, wherever a potluck is held, oven and refrigerator space is likely to be limited, or even nonexistent. Try to choose dishes that can be transported and served at their appropriate temperatures—hot or cold—without last-minute fuss. You'll find plenty of choices in this book.

## Calculating amounts

For most dinners, count on about ¾ pound of bone-in meat (such as turkey, chicken, or ribs) per serving, or ¼ pound of boneless meat, poultry, or fish; and ½ cup of ready-to-eat vegetable, as well as the same amount of potato, rice, or pasta. A typical loaf of bread will serve 6 to 8. Increase all these quantities by about 25 percent to allow for hearty eaters who return for seconds.

If wine will be served, allow 1 bottle (750 ml.) for every 2 or 3 guests at an appetizer party. For a multicourse gourmet dinner, half to two-thirds of a bottle per person may be more realistic. Be sure to offer other beverages as well, such as fruit juice, soft drinks, and bottled water in a variety of flavors. Brew both regular and decaffeinated coffee for after-dinner sipping.

## On the road

To keep food hot, you can purchase an insulated casserole or a quilted cozy to put over one of your own lidded serving dishes or pans. Also, without special equipment, you can insulate any hot dish to maintain its temperature for 2 to 3 hours. First, wrap it in heavy foil, followed by 6 to 8 layers of newspaper. Fasten the paper with tape or string, and carry the bundle in a tightly fitting box, styrofoam chest, or insulated bag. Or nestle it in a quilt or pillows to help to retain its heat.

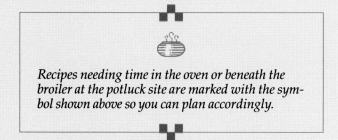

*Recipes needing time in the oven or beneath the broiler at the potluck site are marked with the symbol shown above so you can plan accordingly.*

To keep perishable foods cold during transport, use an insulated cooler or ice chest. Layer ice in the bottom or put containers of solidly frozen artificial refrigerant around the sides and on top of the food.

## Potluck food safety

Everyone has heard of the illnesses that result from spoiled picnic food. Potentially, a potluck can pose the same danger. To play it safe, follow these precautions:

- **Perishable foods** that are especially vulnerable to spoilage include meats, poultry, seafood, eggs, and dairy products, as well as preparations using these foods. Between the temperatures of 50° and 130°F, bacteria thrive in these foods. Avoid highly perishable food if you must travel for a long distance or if the weather is very hot.

- **Cross-contamination** can occur if salmonella are transferred to other foods from raw meat or poultry, which commonly carry the bacteria. Salmonella are easily destroyed by cooking but can cause problems if transmitted to uncooked foods. Thoroughly clean the cutting surface, knife, dish, your hands, or anything else that has contacted raw poultry or meat before touching other foods. After cutting raw meat, poultry, or fish on a board, scrub it with hot, soapy water and rinse it well. Also wipe it occasionally with a solution of household bleach.

- **Keep hot foods hot** by making sure that they're fully heated before packing them for transport. To prevent spoilage, don't hold hot meat, poultry, or fish dishes at a temperature below 140°F for more than 3 hours.

- **Keep cold foods cold** by thoroughly chilling them before packing them for transport. Don't expect a cooler to chill food that isn't cold enough when you pack it. And never transport hot and cold foods together.

- **Put perishable foods away** in a refrigerator or ice chest after everyone has finished at the buffet table. Be especially careful in a warm room or if you're outdoors in hot weather.

## Dinner is served

Experienced potluck cooks know that the best way to show off a prized creation is to use attractive serving dishes and garnishes. Also important are serving utensils, sauces, and condiments. Arrange these on the table near your contribution.

When setting up the buffet, place dishes in a logical sequence where they're easily reached. When the group is large, arrange for self-service from both sides of the table. Another way to handle a crowd is to set out different courses on separate tables, spaced for easy traffic flow.

Once the cooperative effort is ready to serve, everyone can share the rewards of the potluck—great food, fun, and fellowship. For marvelous menu suggestions, recipes, and party ideas for your own potluck adventures, turn to page 7.

### A Word About Our Nutritional Data

*For our recipes, we provide a nutritional analysis stating calorie count; grams of protein, carbohydrates, and total fat; and milligrams of cholesterol and sodium. Generally, the nutritional information applies to a single serving, based on the largest number of servings given for each recipe.*

*The nutritional analysis does not include optional ingredients or those for which no specific amount is stated. If an ingredient is listed with an option, the information was calculated using the first choice. Likewise, if a range is given for the amount of an ingredient, values were figured based on the first, lower amount.*

### 'Tis the Season

*Gather family and friends for a festive holiday brunch featuring (clockwise from upper right) Hot Buttered Cider, squares of Zucchini Frittata, Curried Ham & Rice Rolls, Cranberry Brunch Cake, Old-fashioned Lemon Bread, and a bowl of fresh fruit (menu on facing page).*

# Holiday Cheer

*Pictured on facing page*

Steaming mugs of fragrant spiced cider greet friends as they arrive for this festive brunch. From fruit to freshly baked treats, the menu offers delights for hearty appetites during the holiday season or on any winter's weekend.

**Minted Melon Balls &
Pineapple Chunks
Curried Ham & Rice Rolls
Zucchini Frittata
Cranberry Brunch Cake
Old-fashioned Lemon Bread
Hot Buttered Cider**

With these convenient, make-ahead dishes, only the cider needs last-minute attention. While it heats, warm the mugs by filling them almost to the brim with very hot water.

## Minted Melon Balls & Pineapple Chunks

    1   tablespoon chopped fresh mint or
        1 teaspoon dry mint
    3   tablespoons sugar
    ¼   cup water
    1   cantaloupe (1½ to 2 lbs.)
    1   small honeydew melon (2 to 2½ lbs.)
    1   medium-size pineapple (3 to 3½ lbs.)
        Mint sprig

Place chopped mint in a small heat-proof bowl; set aside.

In a 1-quart pan, combine sugar and water; bring to a boil over high heat, stirring until sugar is dissolved. Boil for 2 minutes; then pour over mint. Cover and refrigerate for 1 hour. Strain syrup, discarding mint; set syrup aside.

Meanwhile, cut cantaloupe and honeydew in half; discard seeds. Using a melon-ball cutter, cut melons into balls. Place in a large glass bowl.

Peel pineapple, discarding rind, top, and core; cut fruit into bite-size chunks. Add to melon. Pour mint syrup over fruit and mix lightly. If made ahead, cover and refrigerate for up to 3 hours. Garnish with mint sprig. Makes 12 servings.

*Per serving: 63 calories, .63 g protein, 16 g carbohydrates, .35 g total fat, 0 mg cholesterol, 7 mg sodium*

## Curried Ham & Rice Rolls

    3   hard-cooked eggs, chopped
    ⅔   cup raisins
    3   cups cooked rice
    3   green onions (including tops), thinly
        sliced
        Salt and pepper
    3   tablespoons butter or margarine
    1   teaspoon curry powder
    2   tablespoons cornstarch
    3   cups milk
    3   packages (4 oz. *each*) cooked ham
        slices (*each* 6 inches long)
        Chopped peanuts

Lightly mix eggs, raisins, rice, and green onions; season to taste with salt and pepper. Set aside.

In a 1½- to 2-quart pan, melt butter over medium heat. Stir in curry powder and cornstarch. Remove from heat and gradually blend in milk. Return to heat and cook, stirring constantly, until sauce boils and thickens. Mix 1½ cups of the sauce into rice mixture; set remaining sauce aside.

Spoon about two-thirds of the rice mixture into a greased 9- by 13-inch baking dish. Dividing remaining rice mixture equally, place a portion at one end of each ham slice; roll to enclose. Arrange ham rolls, seam sides down, in dish and top with remaining sauce. (At this point, you may cover and refrigerate for up to a day.)

Bake, covered, in a 350° oven until hot (about 25 minutes; 35 minutes if refrigerated). Sprinkle with peanuts. Insulate to transport hot (see page 5). Makes 12 servings.

*Per serving: 219 calories, 11 g protein, 23 g carbohydrates, 9 g total fat, 102 mg cholesterol, 503 mg sodium*

## Zucchini Frittata

    2   tablespoons olive oil
    2   tablespoons butter or margarine
    2   medium-size onions, finely chopped
    2   cloves garlic, minced or pressed
    ½   cup chopped parsley
    8   medium-size zucchini (about 2¼ lbs.
        *total*), shredded
    2   tablespoons chopped fresh basil or
        1½ teaspoons dry basil
    ½   cup grated Parmesan cheese
        Salt and pepper
   16   eggs
        Lemon slices

Heat oil and butter in a wide frying pan over medium heat. Add onions, garlic, and parsley; cook, stirring often, until onions are soft (6 to 8 minutes). Add zucchini; cook, stirring, until liquid has evaporated (about 20 minutes). Remove from heat and stir in basil and cheese; season to taste with salt and pepper.

In a large bowl, beat eggs until blended. Stir in zucchini mixture. Spread in a greased shallow 3-quart casserole. Bake, uncovered, in a 350° oven until firm in center when lightly touched (about 45 minutes). Let cool on a wire rack. Cut into serving pieces and arrange on a platter. If made ahead, cover and refrigerate for up to a day. Transport in a cooler.

To serve, garnish with lemon slices. Makes 12 servings.

*Per serving: 176 calories, 11 g protein, 5 g carbohydrates, 13 g total fat, 373 mg cholesterol, 177 mg sodium*

*(Continued on next page)*

## Cranberry Brunch Cake

- **3 cups all-purpose flour**
- **2 teaspoons baking powder**
- **1 teaspoon** *each* **baking soda and ground cinnamon**
- **½ teaspoon ground ginger**
- **¼ teaspoon ground allspice**
- **1 cup (½ lb.) butter or margarine, at room temperature**
- **2 cups granulated sugar**
- **1 tablespoon grated orange peel**
- **3 eggs**
- **1 cup orange juice**
- **1½ cups cranberries**
- **¾ cup chopped walnuts or pecans Powdered sugar**

Stir flour, baking powder, baking soda, cinnamon, ginger, and allspice until well blended; set aside.

In the large bowl of an electric mixer, beat butter, granulated sugar, and orange peel until creamy. Add eggs, one at a time, beating well after each addition. Alternately add flour mixture and orange juice, about a third of each at a time, beating until blended after each addition. With a spoon, stir in cranberries and nuts. Spoon batter into a greased, flour-dusted 10-inch tube pan with a removable bottom.

Bake in a 350° oven until a wooden pick inserted in thickest part comes out clean (about 1 hour). Let cool in pan on a wire rack for 30 minutes. Remove cake from pan and let cool completely.

Before serving, dust with powdered sugar. Makes 12 servings.

*Per serving: 464 calories, 6 g protein, 63 g carbohydrates, 22 g total fat, 110 mg cholesterol, 315 mg sodium*

## Spiced Apple Brunch Cake

Follow directions for **Cranberry Brunch Cake,** but omit cinnamon, ginger, allspice, orange peel, orange juice, and cranberries.

Substitute 2 teaspoons **apple pie spice** for cinnamon, ginger, and allspice; substitute 1 teaspoon **grated lemon peel** for orange peel; substitute 1 cup **apple juice** for orange juice; and substitute 2 medium-size **tart green apples,** peeled, cored, and diced, for cranberries.

## Old-fashioned Lemon Bread

- **1½ cups all-purpose flour**
- **1 cup sugar**
- **1 teaspoon baking powder**
- **½ teaspoon salt**
- **2 eggs**
- **½ cup** *each* **milk and salad oil**
- **1½ teaspoons grated lemon peel Lemon Glaze (recipe follows)**

In a large bowl, stir together flour, sugar, baking powder, and salt. In a small bowl, beat eggs with milk, oil, and lemon peel. Add egg mixture to flour mixture; stir just until blended. Spread batter in a greased, flour-dusted 4½- by 8½-inch loaf pan.

Bake in a 350° oven until a wooden pick inserted in center comes out clean (45 to 50 minutes). Meanwhile, prepare Lemon Glaze.

Using a long wooden skewer, poke numerous holes in hot bread, piercing all the way to bottom. Slowly drizzle hot glaze over bread. Let cool in pan on a wire rack for 15 minutes. Remove from pan and let cool completely on rack. Makes about 12 servings.

**Lemon Glaze.** In a small pan, combine 4½ tablespoons **lemon juice** and ⅓ cup **sugar.** Stir over medium heat until sugar is dissolved.

*Per serving: 243 calories, 3 g protein, 35 g carbohydrates, 10 g total fat, 47 mg cholesterol, 145 mg sodium*

## Hot Buttered Cider

- **3 quarts apple cider**
- **1 tablespoon whole cloves**
- **4 cinnamon sticks (***each* **about 3 inches long)**
- **¾ teaspoon ground nutmeg**
- **¼ cup sugar**
- **2 cups dark rum or additional apple cider**
- **12 pats (about 1 teaspoon** *each***) butter or margarine**

In a 4½- to 5-quart pan, combine cider, cloves, cinnamon sticks, nutmeg, and sugar. Bring to a boil over medium-high heat. Reduce heat and simmer gently, uncovered, for 10 minutes. Pour mixture through a wire strainer into a large bowl; discard spices. Return cider to pan.

Just before serving, reheat until steaming. Stir in rum. Ladle cider into warm mugs and top each with a pat of butter. Makes 12 servings.

*Per serving: 255 calories, .21 g protein, 34 g carbohydrates, 4 g total fat, 10 mg cholesterol, 48 mg sodium*

# Spring Picnic Potluck

When spring fever draws you outdoors for a picnic, here's an elegant menu that's easily portable, whether to the patio or to the park. The strawberry-pear relish complements both the pork roast and the wild rice salad. The tiny artichokes were designed by nature as perfect picnic portions.

**Pork Loin Stuffed with
Two Cheeses
Pickled Strawberries & Pears
Tiny Lemon-scented Artichokes
Wild Rice Salad     French Bread
Raspberry Jam Tart
Gewürztraminer     Apple Juice**

Serve the meat cold so the cheese filling will remain firm. The other dishes can safely be carried and served at room temperature, but the beverages will be most appealing if chilled and carried in a cooler.

## Pork Loin Stuffed with Two Cheeses

- 4 ounces *each* cream cheese and ripened or unripened goat cheese, such as Montrachet or bûcheron
- 1 teaspoon ground dry sage
- ½ teaspoon dry thyme
- 1 boned pork loin end roast (about 3 lbs.)
- 12 to 15 large canned grape leaves, drained
  Lemon wedges (optional)
  Additional grape leaves (optional)

Thoroughly blend cream cheese, goat cheese, ½ teaspoon of the sage, and ¼ teaspoon of the thyme; set aside.

Open roast and place flat, fat side down, on a work surface. Cover with plastic wrap and pound with flat side of a meat mallet until roast measures about 9 by 11 inches. Using the 12 to 15 grape leaves, arrange leaves in a double layer down center of meat, extending leaves beyond ends of roast. Spoon cheese mixture down center of leaves just to ends of roast, filling roast so you can reroll it to its original shape. Fold ends of leaves over filling and then lap leaves over cheese to form a neat roll down center. Roll up meat, enclosing filling closely; securely tie with string at about 2-inch intervals.

Place roast, fat side up, in a 9- by 13-inch pan. Rub remaining ½ teaspoon sage and ¼ teaspoon thyme over surface of roast. Insert a meat thermometer into thickest part of meat (not into filling). Roast in a 375° oven until thermometer reaches 160° (about 1¼ hours). Let cool; then cover and refrigerate for at least 3 hours or for up to a day. Transport in a cooler.

To serve, slice meat ¾ to 1 inch thick. Garnish with lemon wedges and additional grape leaves, if desired. Makes 8 servings.

*Per serving: 489 calories, 32 g protein, 3 g carbohydrates, 38 g total fat, 112 mg cholesterol, 276 mg sodium*

## Pickled Strawberries & Pears

- 2½ cups dry white wine
- 1 tablespoon dry tarragon
- 1 cup sugar
- ¼ cup raspberry vinegar or lemon juice
- 4 cups hulled strawberries
- 2 cans (1 lb. *each*) Bartlett pear halves in light syrup, drained

In a 2- to 3-quart pan, combine wine, tarragon, and sugar. Bring to a boil over high heat, stirring until sugar is dissolved. Remove from heat, add vinegar, and let cool.

Combine strawberries and pears in a 2-quart jar; pour tarragon syrup over fruit. Cover and refrigerate for at least 4 hours or for up to a day. Serve cold or at room temperature. Makes 8 servings.

*Per serving: 189 calories, .87 g protein, 48 g carbohydrates, .35 g total fat, 0 mg cholesterol, 11 mg sodium*

## Tiny Lemon-scented Artichokes

- 16 tiny artichokes (*each* 1¾ to 2 inches in diameter)
- 1 quart water
- ⅓ cup lemon juice
- 4 large cloves garlic, sliced
- 2 tablespoons olive oil or salad oil
- ½ teaspoon *each* salt and coarsely ground pepper

Rinse artichokes well. Pull off and discard tough outer leaves; cut off and discard stems.

In a 3- to 4-quart pan, combine water, lemon juice, garlic, oil, salt, and pepper. Cover and bring to a boil over high heat. Add artichokes; cover, return to a boil, and then reduce heat so water boils gently. Cook until artichoke bottoms are tender when pierced (20 to 25 minutes). Drain and let cool. (At this point, you may cover and refrigerate for up to 2 days.)

Eat bottoms of outer leaves; inner leaves (except tips), fuzzy center, and bottom are also edible. Makes 8 servings.

*Per serving: 75 calories, 3 g protein, 16 g carbohydrates, 1 g total fat, 0 mg cholesterol, 171 mg sodium*

*(Continued on next page)*

### Wild Rice Salad

1½ cups wild rice, rinsed and drained
3 cups regular-strength chicken broth
⅓ cup salad oil
2 tablespoons raspberry or wine vinegar
2 tablespoons finely chopped shallots or mild onion
2 teaspoons Dijon mustard
¼ teaspoon pepper

In a 2- to 3-quart pan, bring rice and broth to a boil over high heat. Reduce heat, cover, and simmer, stirring occasionally, until rice is tender to bite and most of the broth is absorbed (about 50 minutes). Let cool.

In a small bowl, blend oil, vinegar, shallots, mustard, and pepper. Pour over rice and mix lightly. If made ahead, cover and refrigerate for up to 2 days. Serve at room temperature. Makes 8 servings.

*Per serving: 202 calories, 5 g protein, 24 g carbohydrates, 10 g total fat, 0 mg cholesterol, 417 mg sodium*

### Raspberry Jam Tart

1 cup plus 2 tablespoons all-purpose flour
4 tablespoons sugar
⅓ cup cold butter or margarine, cut into chunks
1 egg yolk
½ cup plus 1 tablespoon raspberry jam
⅓ cup (4 oz.) almond paste
3 eggs, separated
¼ teaspoon baking powder
⅛ teaspoon almond extract
1 to 2 tablespoons sliced almonds

In a bowl or food processor, stir together 1 cup of the flour and 2 tablespoons of the sugar. Add butter and rub with your fingers (or whirl in processor) until fine crumbs form. With a fork (or whirling in processor), stir in the 1 egg yolk until dough holds together.

Press dough evenly over bottom and sides of a 10- or 11-inch tart pan with a removable bottom. Bake in a 350° oven until pale gold (10 to 12 minutes). Place pan on a wire rack and spread ½ cup of the jam over bottom of crust.

In a bowl, beat almond paste, the 3 egg yolks, baking powder, almond extract, and remaining 2 tablespoons each flour and sugar until smooth.

Using another bowl and clean beaters, beat egg whites until they hold soft peaks. Beat about half the whites into almond paste mixture and then fold in remaining whites. Lightly spread batter in crust. Spoon remaining 1 tablespoon jam on center of batter and sprinkle with almonds.

Bake in a 350° oven until well browned (about 25 minutes). Let cool in pan on a wire rack. If made ahead, cover lightly and let stand at room temperature for up to 8 hours. Transport in pan.

To serve, remove rim and cut into wedges. Makes 8 servings.

*Per serving: 322 calories, 6 g protein, 42 g carbohydrates, 15 g total fat, 157 mg cholesterol, 122 mg sodium*

### Fresh Apricot-Almond Tart

Follow directions for **Raspberry Jam Tart**, but omit raspberry jam and almond paste. Increase sugar to ½ cup; increase sliced almonds to ⅓ cup.

After crust has baked for 10 to 12 minutes and is cooling on wire rack, arrange 2 cups (about 12 oz.) sliced **fresh apricots** in pastry.

For filling, beat egg yolks, baking powder, almond extract, remaining 2 tablespoons floor, and remaining 6 tablespoons sugar until smooth. Fold in the ⅓ cup sliced almonds after folding in beaten egg whites (omit sprinkling with almonds).

### Springtime Picnic

*On a lovely spring day, set out this alfresco feast: Pork Loin Stuffed with Two Cheeses (at center) surrounded by Tiny Lemon-scented Artichokes, Wild Rice Salad, Pickled Strawberries & Pears, Raspberry Jam Tart, and a crusty baguette (menu on page 9).*

# Pasta Party

Inspired by Italy's abundance of pasta possibilities, this potluck menu invites guests to contribute sauces, salad, bread, wine, and dessert while the host provides freshly-cooked pasta. If you include all five sauces, you'll have enough for about 30 people. Select two or three sauces for a smaller group.

*Spicy Mediterranean Meatballs*
*Chicken Chili Sauce*
*Crunchy Vegetable Sauce*
*Creamy Sausage &*
*Mushroom Sauce*
*Eggplant, Olive & Anchovy Sauce*
*Mixed Green Salad*
*Warm Garlic Bread*
*Fresh Fruits*
*Sour Cream Pound Cake*
*(page 88)*
*Chianti Classico or*
*California Zinfandel*
*Espresso Coffee*

Serve just one type of pasta or offer a selection, such as spaghetti, vermicelli, fettuccine, mostaccioli, and tagliarini. (If you want to serve several pastas, you'll find it easiest to cook just one kind at a time.) For each serving, allow 2 to 3 ounces packaged dried pasta or 3 to 4 ounces fresh pasta.

## Spicy Mediterranean Meatballs

*Pictured on page 3*

Meatball Mixture (recipe follows)
3 tablespoons salad oil
2 medium-size onions, finely chopped
3 cloves garlic, minced or pressed
1 teaspoon *each* minced fresh ginger and ground cumin
1 tablespoon paprika
¼ cup finely chopped fresh cilantro (coriander) or parsley
3 tablespoons red wine vinegar
2 large firm-ripe tomatoes, peeled and chopped
1 can (14½ oz.) regular-strength beef broth
1 beef bouillon cube
1 can (6 oz.) tomato paste
Grated Parmesan cheese

Prepare Meatball Mixture; set meatballs aside.

Heat oil in a wide frying pan over medium-high heat. Add onions and cook, stirring, until onions begin to soften (about 5 minutes). Stir in garlic, ginger, cumin, paprika, cilantro, vinegar, tomatoes, broth, and bouillon cube. Increase heat to high and cook, stirring, until mixture boils.

Add meatballs; reduce heat, cover, and simmer for 1 hour. With a slotted spoon, transfer meatballs to a warm casserole and keep warm. Return heat to high and stir in tomato paste. Cook, stirring, until thickened (about 10 more minutes); pour over meatballs. Insulate to transport hot (see page 5).

Offer cheese to add to taste. Makes 8 servings.

*Meatball Mixture.* Crumble 1½ pounds **lean ground beef** into a large bowl. Add ¼ cup **fine dry bread crumbs, 3 eggs,** and 1 large **onion,** finely chopped; mix well. Sprinkle with ¼ cup finely chopped **fresh cilantro** (coriander) or parsley, ¼ cup finely chopped **fresh mint,** 1 tablespoon **paprika,** 1 teaspoon **salt,** ½ teaspoon **pepper,** and ¼ teaspoon **ground cloves;** mix lightly until thoroughly combined.

Shape into 1-inch balls. (At this point, you may arrange meatballs in a single layer in a shallow baking pan, cover, and refrigerate for up to 8 hours.)

*Per serving: 366 calories, 20 g protein, 13 g carbohydrates, 26 g total fat, 167 mg cholesterol, 841 mg sodium*

## Chicken Chili Sauce

1 frying chicken (3 to 3½ lbs.), quartered
2 tablespoons butter or margarine
1 large onion, finely chopped
2 cloves garlic, minced or pressed
2½ teaspoons chili powder
2 teaspoons ground cumin
3 cans (14 oz. *each*) tomato purée
2 cups (8 oz.) shredded jack cheese

In a 5- to 6-quart pan, combine chicken and enough water to barely cover. Simmer, covered, until meat near thighbone is no longer pink when slashed (30 to 40 minutes). Lift out chicken, reserving broth. When chicken is cool enough to handle, remove and discard skin and bones; tear meat into bite-size pieces.

In a wide frying pan, melt butter over medium heat. Add onion and garlic; cook, stirring, until onion is soft but not browned (6 to 8 minutes). Stir in chili powder, cumin, and tomato purée. Cook, uncovered, stirring occasionally, for 15 minutes; if sauce is too thick, stir in a little of the reserved broth. Add chicken to sauce and cook just until hot (about 5 minutes). Insulate to transport hot (see page 5).

Offer cheese to add to taste. Makes 6 to 8 servings.

*Per serving: 302 calories, 27 g protein, 17 g carbohydrates, 14 g total fat, 90 mg cholesterol, 847 mg sodium*

## Crunchy Vegetable Sauce

8 slices bacon, cut into ½- by 1-inch strips
2 medium-size onions, finely chopped
4 cloves garlic, minced or pressed
1 medium-size red or green bell pepper, seeded and chopped
2 medium-size zucchini, cut into ½-inch cubes
4 large ripe tomatoes, cut into ½-inch cubes
⅔ cup *each* chopped fresh basil and parsley
3 tablespoons olive oil or salad oil
    Salt and pepper
    Grated Parmesan cheese

In a wide frying pan, cook bacon over medium heat until crisp. Lift out, drain, and set aside. Discard all but 3 tablespoons of the drippings. Add onions and garlic to drippings in pan. Cook, stirring, until onions are soft but not browned (6 to 8 minutes).

Increase heat to medium-high and add bell pepper and zucchini; stir until tender-crisp (about 2 minutes). Add tomatoes, basil, parsley, and oil; cook, stirring, until hot. Season to taste with salt and pepper, and sprinkle with bacon. Insulate to transport hot (see page 5).

Offer cheese to add to taste. Makes 6 to 8 servings.

*Per serving: 153 calories, 4 g protein, 8 g carbohydrates, 12 g total fat, 9 mg cholesterol, 136 mg sodium*

## Creamy Sausage & Mushroom Sauce

1 pound mild Italian sausages
¼ cup butter or margarine
½ pound mushrooms, thinly sliced
1 cup whipping cream
½ cup dry white wine
⅛ teaspoon ground nutmeg
½ cup grated Parmesan cheese
    Additional grated Parmesan cheese

Remove casings from sausages; crumble meat. In a wide frying pan, melt butter over medium-high heat. Add sausage and mushrooms; cook, stirring occasionally, until sausage and mushrooms are lightly browned and mushroom liquid has evaporated. Spoon off and discard all but ¼ cup of the drippings, if necessary.

Stir in cream and wine; bring to a boil. Boil gently, stirring often, until sauce is slightly thickened (5 to 8 minutes). Mix in nutmeg and the ½ cup cheese. Insulate to transport hot (see page 5).

Offer additional cheese to add to taste. Makes 6 to 8 servings.

*Per serving: 365 calories, 11 g protein, 3 g carbohydrates, 34 g total fat, 96 mg cholesterol, 578 mg sodium*

## Eggplant, Olive & Anchovy Sauce

¼ cup olive oil or salad oil
1 large eggplant (about 1¼ lbs.), unpeeled, cut into ½-inch cubes
2 cloves garlic, minced or pressed
2 small red or green bell peppers, seeded and diced
¼ cup water
2 tablespoons drained capers
1 cup chopped fresh basil or ¼ cup dry basil
6 to 8 canned anchovy fillets, drained and chopped
¼ to ½ teaspoon crushed red pepper
1 can (16 oz.) pitted ripe olives, drained
6 large ripe tomatoes, peeled, seeded, and coarsely chopped
    Salt

Heat oil in a 5- to 6-quart pan over medium heat. Add eggplant and garlic; cook, stirring constantly, for 1 minute. Stir in bell peppers. Reduce heat to low and add water. Cover and cook until eggplant is tender when pierced (6 to 8 minutes).

Add capers, basil, anchovies, crushed red pepper, olives, and tomatoes. Increase heat to medium-high and bring to a gentle boil. Cook, uncovered, stirring often, until sauce is thickened (15 to 20 minutes). Season to taste with salt. Insulate to transport hot (see page 5). Makes 6 to 8 servings.

*Per serving: 221 calories, 4 g protein, 14 g carbohydrates, 19 g total fat, 2 mg cholesterol, 603 mg sodium*

**Smooth Sophistication**

*This savory trio of spreads invites repeated sampling (clockwise from upper left):*
*Quick Chicken Liver Pâté (page 18), Dried Tomato Torta (page 17), and*
*Belgian Endive & Smoked Salmon Appetizer (facing page).*

# Appetizers

At a potluck, the guest who arrives early, bearing an appetizer, is always assured of a warm welcome. Who doesn't love to nibble tantalizing bites while waiting for dinner to begin? Whether your contribution is cold and crisp or piping hot from the oven, it will probably disappear before the first salad is tossed. In this chapter, you'll find numerous tempting choices to offer before dinner, as a first course, or at a potluck appetizer party.

## Belgian Endive & Smoked Salmon Appetizer

*Pictured on facing page*

*Preparation time: 20 minutes*

*Chilling time: At least 1 hour*

For an elegant wintertime buffet, bring this flavorful smoked salmon dip to scoop up with crisp spears of Belgian endive, usually most reasonably priced in the colder months.

> 1 pound (8 to 10 small heads) Belgian endive
> 1 large package (8 oz.) cream cheese, at room temperature
> ⅓ cup (4 oz.) minced smoked salmon
> ¼ cup sour cream
> 1 tablespoon *each* lime juice and minced onion
> 3 tablespoons chopped fresh dill or 2 teaspoons dill weed
> Dill sprigs (optional)

Rinse endive with cold water; drain. Wrap in paper towels and enclose in a plastic bag; refrigerate for at least 1 hour or for up to 3 days.

In the bowl of an electric mixer, combine cream cheese, salmon, sour cream, lime juice, and onion; beat until well blended and fluffy. Mix in chopped dill. (At this point, you may cover and refrigerate for up to 3 days.)

If spread is firm, let stand at room temperature for about 30 minutes; then beat until fluffy. Mound in a small bowl. Transport spread and endive separately in a cooler.

To serve, place spread on a tray. Garnish with dill sprigs, if desired. Cut or break endive spears from core of each head. Surround bowl with endive spears, tips pointing outward. Makes 8 to 10 servings.

*Per serving: 113 calories, 4 g protein, 3 g carbohydrates, 10 g total fat, 30 mg cholesterol, 163 mg sodium*

# Garden-fresh Bagna Cauda

*Pictured on page 67*

❧

*Preparation time: 40 minutes*

Assertive with garlic, Northern Italy's *bagna cauda* (BAHN-yah COW-dah) is a warm, buttery sauce for fresh vegetables. Before transporting it, combine all the ingredients in the container you'll use for heating and serving the sauce. As it warms, you can arrange the vegetables and bread slices on a platter.

Garden-fresh Vegetables (directions follow)
1 cup (½ lb.) butter or margarine
½ cup olive oil
5 large cloves garlic, minced or pressed
2 tablespoons lemon juice
1½ teaspoons pepper
2 cans (2 oz. *each*) anchovy fillets
Thinly sliced French bread

Prepare Garden-fresh Vegetables. Set aside.

In a 3- to 4-cup heatproof container, combine butter, oil, garlic, lemon juice, and pepper. Drain oil from anchovies into butter mixture; finely chop anchovies and add to container. Transport vegetables and container of sauce separately in a cooler.

Place sauce over medium heat until butter is melted. Keep warm over a candle or alcohol flame, or reheat periodically; sauce may brown slightly, but check occasionally to be sure butter doesn't burn. Present vegetables alongside.

To eat, swirl vegetables through hot sauce; hold a slice of bread underneath to catch drips, or use bread for dipping. Makes 16 to 20 servings.

*Garden-fresh Vegetables.* Choose a colorful assortment of tiny **yellow pear and cherry tomatoes; pattypan squash; golden or green zucchini; yellow crookneck squash; green, red, yellow, and purple bell peppers; baby carrots; green onions; broccoli;** and **cauliflower.** Rinse vegetables well and drain. Cut, if necessary, into dipping-size pieces; but try to retain natural shape of larger vegetables as much as possible—for example, loosen flowerets from cauliflower core, but keep within a few outer leaves. Allow 1 to 2 cups vegetables per person.

*Per tablespoon sauce: 90 calories, 1 g protein, .32 g carbohydrate, 9 g total fat, 17 mg cholesterol, 189 mg sodium*

# Bell Peppers with Peppercorn Dip

❧

*Preparation time: 25 minutes*

A colorful bell pepper shell—purple, red, or yellow—holds a green peppercorn–seasoned mayonnaise dip for bell pepper strips. To prevent spills, fill the hollowed-out peppers with the dip after you arrive at the potluck.

½ cup mayonnaise
1 clove garlic
¼ cup sliced green onions (including tops)
1 tablespoon *each* green peppercorns (dry or drained canned) and white wine vinegar
2 medium-size whole purple, red, or yellow bell peppers (*each* about 2½ inches tall)
3 or 4 medium-size purple, red, or yellow bell peppers, seeded and cut into ¼-inch strips

In a blender or food processor, combine mayonnaise, garlic, green onions, green peppercorns, and vinegar; whirl until smooth. (At this point, you may cover and refrigerate for up to a day.)

Cut out and set aside stem ends of the 2 bell peppers. Remove seeds. Trim bottoms slightly, if needed, so peppers can stand upright. Transport pepper shells, sauce, and pepper strips separately in a cooler.

Fill peppers with sauce; replace tops, if desired. Serve pepper strips alongside to dip into sauce. Makes about 10 servings.

*Per serving: 88 calories, .46 g protein, 2 g carbohydrates, 9 g total fat, 6 mg cholesterol, 64 mg sodium*

# Vegetable-Cheese Nachos

*Pictured on page 19*

❧

*Preparation time: 25 minutes*

*Broiling time: 5 to 7 minutes*

Instead of tortilla chips, offer crisp raw vegetables as the base for this colorful melted cheese appetizer. Arrange everything on a heatproof platter to transport; then broil briefly just before serving.

4 cups raw vegetables (carrot or celery sticks, zucchini or crookneck squash slices, green or red bell pepper strips, jicama or turnip sticks or slices)

2 cups (8 oz.) shredded jack or Cheddar cheese

2 to 3 tablespoons *each* canned diced green chiles and sliced ripe olives

Arrange vegetables (choose some or all from those suggested) on a large heatproof platter. Top evenly with cheese, chiles, and olives. Transport in a cooler.

Broil 4 to 6 inches below heat until cheese is melted (5 to 7 minutes). Use vegetables to scoop up topping. Makes about 6 servings.

*Per serving: 177 calories, 10 g protein, 7 g carbohydrates, 12 g total fat, 33 mg cholesterol, 271 mg sodium*

# Chile-Cheese Spread

*Preparation time: 10 minutes*

*Chilling time: At least 8 hours*

Bring along several kinds of snack crackers to serve with this brandied cheese spread enlivened with green chiles. For a milder impact, substitute pimentos or green onions for the chiles.

1 small package (3 oz.) cream cheese, at room temperature

4 cups (1 lb.) shredded sharp Cheddar cheese, at room temperature

1 tablespoon olive oil

1 teaspoon *each* garlic salt and dry mustard

2 tablespoons brandy

½ cup canned diced green chiles, chopped pimentos, or thinly sliced green onions (including tops)

In the large bowl of an electric mixer, combine cream cheese and Cheddar cheese. Add oil, garlic salt, mustard, and brandy; beat until smooth. Mix in chiles. Cover and refrigerate for at least 8 hours or for up to 6 weeks. Transport in a cooler.

Let stand at room temperature for about 1 hour until softened; mix well before serving. Makes about 2¾ cups.

*Per tablespoon spread: 53 calories, 3 g protein, .29 g carbohydrate, 4 g total fat, 13 mg cholesterol, 121 mg sodium*

# Dried Tomato Torta

*Pictured on page 14*

*Preparation time: 25 minutes*

*Chilling time: About 20 minutes*

*Baking time: About 5 minutes*

Sun-dried tomatoes explain the bold color and unique flavor of this rich cheese spread. For a festive presentation, wreathe the torta with fresh basil leaves and dried tomato ribbons. Serve with triangles of crisp, toasted pocket bread.

Pocket Bread Toast Triangles (directions follow)

1 large package (8 oz.) cream cheese, at room temperature

1 cup (½ lb.) unsalted butter, at room temperature

1 cup (about 5 oz.) freshly grated Parmesan cheese

½ cup dried tomatoes packed in oil, drained (reserve oil)

2 tablespoons oil from dried tomatoes packed in oil

About 2 cups lightly packed fresh basil leaves

Prepare Pocket Bread Toast Triangles. Set aside.

With an electric mixer or food processor, beat cream cheese, butter, and Parmesan cheese until very smoothly blended.

Cut 4 of the tomatoes into thin strips; set aside. In a blender or food processor, whirl remaining tomatoes, oil, and about ½ cup of the cheese mixture until tomatoes are very smoothly puréed. Add purée mixture to cheese mixture and beat until blended. Cover and refrigerate for about 20 minutes or until firm enough to shape.

Mound cheese on a platter. (At this point, you may cover with an inverted bowl and refrigerate for up to 3 days.) Transport cheese, reserved tomato strips, and basil separately in a cooler.

To serve, arrange reserved tomato strips and basil around torta; present with toast triangles. To eat, spread cheese on toast; top with a basil leaf and a tomato strip. Makes 8 to 10 servings.

*Pocket Bread Toast Triangles.* Split 6 rounds **pocket bread** (6 inches in diameter) in half. Cut each round into 6 triangles. Place in a single layer on 2 baking sheets. Bake in a 400° oven for 3 minutes. Switch pan positions and continue baking until lightly toasted (about 2 more minutes). Let cool. If made ahead, store airtight for up to 3 days.

*Per serving: 473 calories, 11 g protein, 27 g carbohydrates, 37 g total fat, 84 mg cholesterol, 775 mg sodium*

## Quick Chicken Liver Pâté

*Pictured on page 14*

◼

*Preparation time: 8 minutes*

*Cooking time: About 10 minutes*

*Chilling time: At least 3 hours*

Present this herbed spread in a crock or terrine, with a basket of baguette slices alongside.

 2 teaspoons butter or margarine
 3 green onions (including tops), thinly sliced
 1 pound chicken livers
 ½ cup dry red wine
 ¼ teaspoon salt
 ⅛ teaspoon *each* dry thyme and pepper
 2 tablespoons chopped parsley
 1 cup (½ lb.) butter or margarine, diced, at room temperature
   Additional chopped parsley (optional)

In a wide frying pan, melt the 2 teaspoons butter over medium-high heat. Add green onions; cook, stirring, until limp. Add chicken livers; cook, turning, until browned. Stir in wine, salt, thyme, and pepper; reduce heat and simmer, uncovered, for 3 minutes. Add the 2 tablespoons parsley.

Transfer mixture to a food processor or blender. Whirl until smooth. With motor running, drop in butter pieces, a few at a time, and whirl until well combined. Cover and refrigerate for at least 3 hours or for up to 4 days. Garnish with additional parsley, if desired. Transport in a cooler. Makes about 3 cups.

*Per tablespoon pâté: 48 calories, 2 g protein, .42 g carbohydrate, 4 g total fat, 52 mg cholesterol, 60 mg sodium*

## Chili Chicken Chunks

*Pictured on facing page*

◼

*Preparation time: 30 minutes*

*Cooking time: About 15 minutes*

Bite-size chunks of boneless chicken, piquantly seasoned with chili powder, serve as dippers for guacamole.

   Guacamole (recipe follows)
 3 whole chicken breasts (about 1 lb. *each*), split; 9 chicken thighs (about 3 lbs. *total*); or half of each
 ¾ cup all-purpose flour
 ¼ cup yellow cornmeal
 2 teaspoons chili powder
 ½ teaspoon *each* paprika and salt
 ¼ teaspoon *each* ground cumin and dry oregano
 ⅛ teaspoon pepper
 ¾ cup beer
   Salad oil

Prepare Guacamole.

Skin and bone chicken. Cut into 1- to 1½-inch chunks and set aside. In a bowl, mix flour, cornmeal, chili powder, paprika, salt, cumin, oregano, and pepper. Add beer and stir until smooth.

Add chicken pieces to batter (if using a combination of light and dark meat, keep them in separate bowls and add an equal amount of batter to each). Stir chicken to coat evenly.

In a deep 3- to 4-quart pan, pour oil to a depth of 1 to 1½ inches and heat to 350°F on a deep-frying thermometer. Lift chicken from batter, a piece at a time, and add to oil. Fill pan with a single layer of chicken (do not crowd). Cook, stirring occasionally, until chicken is richly browned and no longer pink in center when cut (about 2 minutes for breast pieces, 3 minutes for thigh pieces).

Lift out cooked chicken with a slotted spoon and drain on paper towels; let cool. If made ahead, cover and refrigerate for up to a day. Transport chicken and dip separately in a cooler.

Reheat chicken in a paper towel–lined pan in a 350° oven until hot (about 15 minutes). Mound in a napkin-lined basket; serve with guacamole. Makes 8 to 10 servings.

*Guacamole.* Pit, peel, and mash 2 medium-size ripe **avocados.** Blend in ¼ cup **sour cream** or plain yogurt, 2 tablespoons **lime juice** or lemon juice, 2 tablespoons chopped **fresh cilantro** (coriander), ½ teaspoon **ground cumin,** and 2 to 4 tablespoons **canned diced green chiles.** Season to taste with **salt** and **liquid hot pepper seasoning.** If made ahead, cover and refrigerate for up to a day; stir before serving. Makes about 2 cups.

*Per serving chicken: 221 calories, 22 g protein, 11 g carbohydrates, 9 g total fat, 51 mg cholesterol, 173 mg sodium*

*Per tablespoon Guacamole: 25 calories, .29 g protein, 1 g carbohydrate, 2 g total fat, .79 mg cholesterol, 9 mg sodium*

**Life of the Party**

*Sure to please any crowd are these hot and spicy finger foods: at top, golden
Chili Chicken Chunks with guacamole (facing page); below, colorful
Vegetable-Cheese Nachos (page 16).*

# Artichoke Hearts with Blue Cheese

*Pictured on page 62*

◆◆

*Preparation time: 30 minutes*

*Baking time: About 10 minutes*

Artichoke hearts crowned with tangy blue cheese add up to a mouthful of flavor. Arrange the tidy morsels in a baking dish and transport in an insulated container. Bake briefly just before serving.

- 2 **quarts water**
- 2 **tablespoons vinegar or lemon juice**
- 12 **small artichokes (*each* 2 inches in diameter) or 2 packages (10 oz. *each*) frozen artichoke hearts, thawed**
- ¼ **cup butter or margarine, at room temperature**
- 3 **ounces (about ½ cup) blue-veined cheese, crumbled**

Combine water and vinegar in a 5- to 6-quart pan. Remove and discard coarse outer leaves of artichokes down to tender, pale yellow leaves. Snip off thorny tips of remaining leaves; trim stems to about ½ inch. (Or use 24 frozen artichoke halves.) As artichokes are trimmed, drop into water.

Bring water to a boil over high heat; reduce heat, cover, and simmer until artichoke bottoms are tender when pierced (10 to 15 minutes for either fresh or frozen artichokes). Drain; let cool. Cut whole artichokes in half lengthwise.

Arrange artichoke halves, cut sides up, in an ungreased baking dish. In a small bowl, combine butter and cheese; mash with a fork until well com-

bined. Spoon mixture into centers of artichoke halves. (At this point, you may cover and refrigerate for up to a day.) Transport in a cooler.

Bake, uncovered, in a 350° oven just until cheese is melted (about 10 minutes). Serve hot. Makes 24 appetizers.

*Per appetizer: 39 calories, 1 g protein, 2 g carbohydrates, 3 g total fat, 8 mg cholesterol, 80 mg sodium*

# Melted Brie in Crust

◆◆

*Preparation time: 15 minutes*

*Baking time: About 20 minutes*

Few guests can resist a taste of velvety Brie, melted inside a warm, crusty loaf of French bread. It's an easy appetizer that stays warm for up to an hour after serving. Wait until you arrive at the party to bake it.

- 1 **round or oval loaf (about 1 lb.) day-old French bread**
- ⅓ **cup olive oil or melted butter or margarine**
- 2 **cloves garlic, minced or pressed**
- 1 **to 1½ pounds Brie, Camembert, or St. André cheese**

With a serrated knife, cut down through top of bread to leave a shell about ½ inch thick on sides; do not cut through bottom crust. Slide your fingers down toward center of loaf and pull free in a single piece, leaving about a ½-inch-thick base in shell. Around rim of shell, make cuts 1½ inches deep and 1½ inches apart. Slice bread from center of loaf into ½-inch-thick slices; set aside.

Mix oil and garlic. Brush inside of shell with about 3 tablespoons of the oil mixture; brush bread slices with remaining mixture. Place cheese with rind (or trim and discard rind, if desired) in bread shell, cutting into chunks, if necessary, to fit.

Arrange filled shell and bread slices in a single layer in a shallow rimmed baking pan. Cover with foil to transport.

Bake, uncovered, in a 350° oven until bread slices are toasted (about 10 minutes). Remove slices and place around edge of a tray. Continue baking cheese-filled shell until cut edge of bread is golden and cheese is melted (about 10 more minutes).

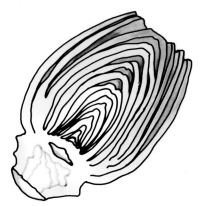

Place cheese-filled shell on tray with toasted bread slices to dip into melted cheese. Makes 10 to 12 servings.

*Per serving: 352 calories, 15 g protein, 21 g carbohydrates, 23 g total fat, 58 mg cholesterol, 576 mg sodium*

# Cranberry Cocktail Meatballs

*Preparation time: 25 minutes*

*Baking time: 5 to 7 minutes*

Baking these bite-size meatballs in a very hot oven, rather than sautéing them, takes some of the work out of preparing this colorful appetizer. While in transit, the meatballs will absorb the flavors of the cranberry sauce.

  2  **pounds ground lean beef**
  1  **cup cornflake crumbs**
  ⅓  **cup finely chopped parsley**
  2  **eggs**
  ¼  **teaspoon pepper**
  1  **clove garlic, minced or pressed**
  ⅓  **cup catsup**
  2  **tablespoons** *each* **thinly sliced green onions (including tops) and soy sauce**
  1  **can (1 lb.) whole berry cranberry sauce**
  1  **bottle (12 oz.) tomato-based chili sauce**
  1  **tablespoon** *each* **brown sugar and lemon juice**

In a large bowl, combine beef, cornflake crumbs, parsley, eggs, pepper, garlic, catsup, green onions, and soy sauce. Mix thoroughly; then shape into 1-inch balls. Arrange, slightly apart, in ungreased shallow 10- by 15-inch rimmed baking pans. Bake, uncovered, in a 500° oven until lightly browned (5 to 7 minutes).

Meanwhile, in a 2- to 3-quart pan, combine cranberry sauce, chili sauce, sugar, and lemon juice. Place over medium heat and stir until melted and bubbling (about 3 minutes).

With a slotted spoon, transfer cooked meatballs to a casserole dish; pour sauce over meatballs. Insulate to transport hot (see page 5).

Serve on a warming tray to keep meatballs hot. Offer picks for spearing. Makes about 75 appetizers.

*Per appetizer: 48 calories, 3 g protein, 5 g carbohydrates, 2 g total fat, 14 mg cholesterol, 128 mg sodium*

# Pistachio-Turkey Appetizer Cups

*Preparation time: 45 minutes*

*Baking time: 12 to 15 minutes*

Mushroom caps laden with a minty ground turkey and pistachio stuffing become savory and substantial morsels when served as an appetizer. They'll taste freshest if you wait until you reach the potluck to bake them.

 40  **mushrooms, 1½ to 2 inches in diameter (about 2 lbs.** *total***)**
  3  **tablespoons soy sauce**
  1  **tablespoon olive oil or salad oil**
  1  **small onion, finely chopped**
  ½  **cup finely chopped salted pistachios**
  ½  **pound ground turkey**
  1  **tablespoon cornstarch**
  1  **egg white**
  3  **tablespoons fine dry bread crumbs**
  ¼  **cup chopped fresh mint**

Rinse mushrooms and pat dry. Carefully break off stems; mince stems and set aside.

Arrange a third of the mushrooms, cup sides up, in a wide frying pan. Add 1 tablespoon of the soy sauce and cook over medium heat until cups contain liquid (3 to 4 minutes); turn mushrooms and cook until pan is almost dry (about 3 more minutes). Transfer mushrooms, cup sides up, to an oiled 9- by 13-inch baking dish. Repeat, using remaining soy sauce, until all mushrooms are cooked.

To same pan add oil, onion, and minced mushroom stems. Cook over medium-high heat, stirring often, until onion is soft and mixture is dry. Add pistachios and stir until mixture is lightly browned; remove from heat and let cool.

To onion mixture add turkey, cornstarch, egg white, bread crumbs, and mint; mix well. Divide mixture into 40 equal portions and shape each into a ball. Set a ball in each mushroom cap and press down to settle firmly in place. (At this point, you may cover and refrigerate for up to a day.) Transport in a cooler.

Bake mushrooms, uncovered, in a 500° oven until turkey is no longer pink in center when cut (12 to 15 minutes). Serve hot. Makes 40 appetizers.

*Per appetizer: 32 calories, 2 g protein, 2 g carbohydrates, 2 g total fat, 4 mg cholesterol, 101 mg sodium.*

### Mediterranean Holiday

*To accompany roast leg of lamb, a Middle Eastern tradition, let guests bring*
*(from left) Bulgur & Rice Pilaf (page 41), Chard, Feta & Fila Pie (page 39), and*
*Greek Peasant Salad (facing page).*

# Salads & Vegetables

■■

How do enthusiasts approach a potluck? They sample a little of this and a little of that from its entire diversity of dishes. Much of the tempting variety shows up as salads and vegetables, menu categories that cover everything from crisp, leafy salads to fluffy rice casseroles and from marinated garden vegetables to cheese-gilded potatoes. At home, you'd probably have only one or two choices to accompany your baked ham or turkey. At a potluck, why not try a spoonful of each—especially if the recipes come from this chapter.

## Greek Peasant Salad

*Pictured on facing page*

■■

*Preparation time: 25 minutes*

Bathed in a simple olive oil and lemon juice dressing, this crisp vegetable salad makes a sensational accompaniment to barbecued meats or chicken at a summer potluck. Or, in cold weather, serve it alongside a simple stew or casserole, such as Molded Moussaka (page 82).

  **Lemon Dressing (recipe follows)**
 1 **quart loosely packed torn chicory (curly endive) leaves, washed and crisped**
 2 **large tomatoes, cut into bite-size chunks**
 1 **large green bell pepper, seeded and cut into 1-inch squares**
 1 **cup peeled cucumber slices**
 1 **small red onion, sliced and separated into rings**
 ¼ **pound blue-veined or feta cheese, crumbled**
 12 **to 18 Greek-style olives**

Prepare Lemon Dressing; set aside.

In a 3- to 4-quart bowl, layer chicory, tomatoes, bell pepper, cucumber, red onion, cheese, and olives, using all of each ingredient for each layer. (At this point, you may cover and refrigerate for up to 4 hours.) Transport salad in a cooler.

To serve, stir dressing, pour over salad, and mix lightly until well coated. Makes 6 servings.

*Lemon Dressing.* Combine 2 tablespoons **lemon juice,** ¼ cup **olive oil,** 2 tablespoons **salad oil,** and ¾ teaspoon **dry oregano.** Mix until well blended.

*Per serving: 237 calories, 6 g protein, 11 g carbohydrates, 20 g total fat, 17 mg cholesterol, 468 mg sodium*

## Spinach Salad with Basil Dressing

*Pictured on page 62 and front cover*

◼◼

*Preparation time: 25 minutes*

A fresh basil dressing lends spirit to this spinach salad. Assemble it ahead of time, mixing in the dressing just before serving.

   Basil Dressing (recipe follows)
¾ pound spinach, rinsed well
8 to 10 medium-size mushrooms, thinly sliced
1 small red onion, thinly sliced and separated into rings
2 hard-cooked eggs, shredded, or ½ cup (about 4 oz.) crumbled Gorgonzola or other blue-veined cheese
½ cup roasted salted sunflower seeds (optional)

Prepare Basil Dressing; set aside.

   Pat spinach dry, remove stems, and tear into bite-size pieces. In a large salad bowl, combine spinach, mushrooms, red onion, and eggs. (At this point, you may cover and refrigerate for up to 4 hours.) Transport salad in a cooler.

   To serve, stir dressing, pour over salad, and mix lightly until well coated. Sprinkle with sunflower seeds, if desired. Makes 6 servings.

***Basil Dressing.*** In a medium-size bowl, combine 2 cloves **garlic,** minced or pressed, and 3 tablespoons finely chopped **fresh basil leaves** or 2½ teaspoons dry basil; mash with back of a spoon until well blended. Stir in ¼ cup **red wine vinegar** and ½ cup **olive oil** or salad oil.

*Per serving: 310 calories, 8 g protein, 7 g carbohydrates, 29 g total fat, 14 mg cholesterol, 381 mg sodium*

## Overnight Layered Green Salad

◼◼

*Preparation time: 45 minutes*

*Chilling time: At least 8 hours*

Creamy dressing, chopped eggs, and crisp bacon top layers of shredded lettuce and crunchy vegetables in this popular salad. You can make it as much as a day ahead of the potluck.

1 medium-size head iceberg lettuce (about 1 lb.), washed and crisped
½ cup thinly sliced green onions (including tops)
1 cup thinly sliced celery
1 can (8 oz.) sliced water chestnuts, drained
1 package (10 oz.) frozen tiny peas
   Lemon-Garlic Mayonnaise (recipe follows)
½ cup grated Parmesan cheese
3 hard-cooked eggs, shredded
½ pound sliced bacon, crisply cooked and crumbled
2 medium-size tomatoes, cut into wedges

Shred lettuce and place in a 3- to 4-quart serving bowl. Top with layers of green onions, celery, water chestnuts, and frozen peas, using all of each ingredient for each layer.

   Prepare Lemon-Garlic Mayonnaise and spread evenly over salad; sprinkle with cheese. Cover and refrigerate for at least 8 hours or for up to a day.

   Sprinkle salad with eggs and bacon. Arrange tomatoes around edge of bowl. Transport in a cooler. To serve, use a spoon and fork to lift out some of each layer. Makes 8 to 10 servings.

***Lemon-Garlic Mayonnaise.*** Combine 1½ cups **mayonnaise;** 1 tablespoon **Dijon mustard;** 1 clove **garlic,** minced or pressed; ¼ cup **lemon juice;** and ¼ teaspoon **pepper.** Mix until smoothly blended. Makes about 1¾ cups.

*Per serving: 365 calories, 8 g protein, 11 g carbohydrates, 33 g total fat, 110 mg cholesterol, 487 mg sodium*

## Cauliflower & Zucchini with Tahini

◼◼

*Preparation time: 20 minutes*

*Cooking time: About 15 minutes*

Always popular at a potluck are lightly cooked fresh vegetables, such as cauliflowerets and sliced zucchini arranged decoratively on a platter. Drizzle with an irresistible dressing of lemony yogurt and tahini just before serving.

   Tahini Sauce (recipe follows)
1 medium-size cauliflower (about 1 lb.)
4 medium-size zucchini (about 1 lb. *total*)
   Parsley sprigs
   Lemon slices

Prepare Tahini Sauce; set aside.

Break cauliflowerets from core; discard core and leaves. Trim and discard ends of zucchini; slice about ½ inch thick.

In a 4- to 5-quart pan, bring 3 quarts water to a boil over high heat. Add cauliflowerets and cook, uncovered, until tender when pierced (6 to 8 minutes). Lift vegetables out with a slotted spoon, drain, and arrange on one side of a large serving platter.

Add zucchini to boiling water and cook, uncovered, until tender when pierced (4 to 6 minutes). Drain, immerse in cold water until cool, and drain again. Arrange zucchini on other side of platter. (At this point, you may cover and refrigerate for up to a day; drain and discard any liquid that accumulates on platter.) Transport salad and sauce in a cooler.

To serve, stir sauce and pour over vegetables. Garnish with parsley and lemon. Makes 8 servings.

*Tahini Sauce.* Drain and reserve liquid from 1 small can (8¾ oz.) **garbanzo beans.** In a blender or food processor, combine beans, ½ cup *each* **plain yogurt** and **lemon juice,** ½ cup **canned tahini** (sesame seed paste), ½ teaspoon **ground cumin,** and 1 clove **garlic;** whirl until smoothly puréed. Blend in just enough of the reserved bean liquid to make sauce pourable. Season to taste with **salt** and **pepper.** If made ahead, cover and refrigerate for up to a week.

*Per serving: 152 calories, 6 g protein, 15 g carbohydrates, 9 g total fat, .85 mg cholesterol, 128 mg sodium*

## Tarragon-marinated Vegetable Platter

*Pictured on page 94*

◼ ◼

*Preparation time: 15 minutes*

*Cooking time: About 20 minutes*

*Chilling time: At least 4 hours*

Colorful marinated vegetables in a mustardy tarragon vinaigrette can serve as either a salad or a vegetable. Since you can prepare the entire dish as much as 24 hours ahead, there's no last-minute fuss.

1  **large cauliflower (1½ to 1¾ lbs.)**
4  **large carrots**
1  **package (9 oz.) frozen artichoke hearts, thawed**
2  **cups cherry tomatoes**
   **Tarragon Dressing (recipe follows)**

Break cauliflowerets from core; discard core and leaves. Cut cauliflower pieces in half lengthwise, if necessary, to make them all about the same size. Slice carrots diagonally about ¼ inch thick. Place cauliflower, carrots, and artichokes separately on a rack over about 1 inch boiling water. Cover and steam until barely tender when pierced (7 to 10 minutes for cauliflower; 4 to 6 minutes each for carrots and artichokes). As each vegetable is cooked, immerse in cold water until cool; drain well.

Arrange cooked vegetables and tomatoes in separate rows in a 9- by 13-inch dish or rimmed serving platter.

Prepare Tarragon Dressing and pour over all. Cover and refrigerate for at least 4 hours or for up to a day. Transport in a cooler. Makes 6 to 8 servings.

*Tarragon Dressing.* Combine ⅔ cup **olive oil** or salad oil; ⅓ cup **tarragon vinegar** or white wine vinegar; 1 clove **garlic,** minced or pressed; 1½ tablespoons **Dijon mustard;** 1¼ teaspoons **salt;** 1 teaspoon **dry tarragon;** and ½ teaspoon **pepper.** Mix until well blended.

*Per serving: 214 calories, 2 g protein, 12 g carbohydrates, 19 g total fat, 0 mg cholesterol, 466 mg sodium*

## Marinated Broccoli & Mushrooms

*Pictured on facing page*

■

*Preparation time: 15 minutes*

*Cooking time: 3 minutes*

*Chilling time: 1 to 2 hours*

Celery seeds accent the dressing drizzled over this cool salad of briefly steamed broccoli and crisp raw mushrooms, onions, and celery. For freshest colors and textures, make the salad within 2 hours of serving.

- 1½ **pounds broccoli**
- ¾ **pound mushrooms, thinly sliced**
- 1 **cup** *each* **thinly sliced green onions (including tops) and thinly sliced celery**
- ¼ **cup sugar**
- ⅓ **cup cider vinegar**
- 1 **teaspoon** *each* **paprika and celery seeds**
- 1 **cup salad oil**
  **Salt and pepper**

Trim and discard broccoli stem ends and, if desired, peel stalks. Cut flowerets from stalks, separating into bite-size pieces. Cut stalks diagonally into ¼-inch-thick slices. Place broccoli on a rack over about 1 inch boiling water. Cover and steam until barely tender when pierced (about 2 minutes). Immerse in cold water until cool; drain well.

In a large bowl, combine broccoli, mushrooms, green onions, and celery. In a small bowl, stir together sugar and vinegar until sugar is dissolved; add paprika, celery seeds, and oil. Mix until well blended.

Pour dressing over vegetables; mix lightly until well coated. Cover and refrigerate, stirring occasionally, for 1 to 2 hours. Transport in a cooler. Offer salt and pepper to add to taste. Makes 6 to 8 servings.

*Per serving: 299 calories, 3 g protein, 13 g carbohydrates, 28 g total fat, 0 mg cholesterol, 30 mg sodium*

## White Bean & Cherry Tomato Salad

*Pictured on facing page*

■

*Preparation time: 15 minutes*

*Cooking time: 2 hours*

*Chilling time: At least 6 hours*

At a summertime barbecue, this herbed bean salad, brightened with cherry tomatoes, makes an appetizing potluck contribution.

- 1 **pound small white beans, rinsed and drained**
- 1 **teaspoon salt**
- 2 **tablespoons white wine vinegar**
- 1 **tablespoon Dijon mustard**
- 4 **drops liquid hot pepper seasoning**
- ⅓ **cup salad oil**
- 2 **tablespoons chopped fresh basil leaves or 2 teaspoons dry basil**
- 1½ **teaspoons chopped fresh mint leaves or ½ teaspoon dry mint**
- 3 **tablespoons** *each* **chopped parsley and green onions (including tops)**
- 1 **small clove garlic, minced or pressed**
  **Salt and pepper**
- 1 **basket (about 2 cups) cherry tomatoes, halved**
  **Mint sprigs**

In a 4- to 5-quart pan, bring 2 quarts water to a boil over high heat. Add beans and cook, uncovered, for 2 minutes. Remove from heat, cover, and let stand for 1 hour. Drain beans, discarding water.

In same pan, combine 6 cups water and the 1 teaspoon salt; bring to a boil over high heat. Add beans and cook, partially covered, until tender (about 1 hour). Drain and set aside.

In a medium-size bowl, combine vinegar, mustard, and hot pepper seasoning. Beating with a whisk, slowly add oil; set dressing aside.

In a large bowl, combine beans, basil, chopped mint, parsley, green onions, and garlic. Mix in dressing. Season to taste with salt and pepper. Cover and refrigerate for at least 6 hours or for up to a day. Transport salad, tomatoes, and mint sprigs separately in a cooler.

To serve, lightly mix tomatoes into salad; garnish with mint. Makes 8 to 10 servings.

*Per serving: 223 calories, 11 g protein, 29 g carbohydrates, 8 g total fat, 0 mg cholesterol, 275 mg sodium*

### Garden Party Menu

*Present barbecued chicken and freshly baked muffins. Then add a chorus of cool side dishes (from left): White Bean & Cherry Tomato Salad (facing page), Crunchy Vegetable & Bulgur Salad (page 32), and Marinated Broccoli & Mushrooms (facing page).*

## Mustard-dressed Pea Salad

*Preparation time: 10 minutes*

*Cooking time: 8 to 10 minutes*

Crumbled bacon, chopped onion, and sliced mushrooms all contribute to this piquant pea salad.

- ½ **cup** *each* **sour cream and mayonnaise**
- 1½ **tablespoons Dijon mustard**
- 2½ **tablespoons white wine vinegar**
- ½ **teaspoon** *each* **dry tarragon and ground nutmeg**
- 6 **or 7 slices bacon**
- 1 **small onion, finely chopped**
- ¼ **pound mushrooms, thinly sliced**
- 3 **packages (10 oz.** *each)* **frozen tiny peas, thawed**
    **Lettuce leaves, washed and crisped**
    **Salt and pepper**

Mix sour cream, mayonnaise, mustard, vinegar, tarragon, and nutmeg. (At this point, you may cover and refrigerate for up to a day.)

In a wide frying pan, cook bacon over medium heat until crisp. Lift out, drain, crumble, and set aside; discard all but 3 tablespoons of the drippings. Add onion to drippings and cook, stirring occasionally, until limp. Add mushrooms and continue cooking, stirring occasionally, just until mushrooms are soft. Transfer to a large bowl and stir in peas. (At this point, you may cover and refrigerate vegetables for up to 4 hours.) Transport vegetables, dressing, and bacon separately in a cooler.

Pour dressing over pea mixture. Tuck lettuce around salad; sprinkle with bacon. Offer salt and pepper to add to taste. Makes 6 to 8 servings.

*Per serving: 274 calories, 8 g protein, 15 g carbohydrates, 21 g total fat, 22 mg cholesterol, 419 mg sodium*

## Pea & Roasted Pecan Slaw

*Preparation time: 12 to 15 minutes*

This simple, traditional salad is a perfect accompaniment for fried chicken and hot biscuits.

- 1 **package (10 oz.) frozen tiny peas, thawed**
- 2 **cups finely shredded green cabbage**
- 3 **green onions (including tops), thinly sliced**
- ¼ **cup** *each* **sour cream and mayonnaise**

- 1 **tablespoon white wine vinegar**
- 1 **teaspoon Dijon mustard**
- ¼ **teaspoon curry powder**
- 5 **to 7 romaine lettuce leaves, washed and crisped**
- 1 **cup dry-roasted pecan halves**
    **Salt**

In a large bowl, combine peas, cabbage, and green onions. In a small bowl, combine sour cream, mayonnaise, vinegar, mustard, and curry powder; mix until well blended. (At this point, you may cover and refrigerate salad and dressing separately for up to a day.) Transport salad, dressing, and lettuce separately in a cooler.

Mix in dressing and half the pecans. Season to taste with salt. Garnish with lettuce and remaining ½ cup pecans. Makes 6 servings.

*Per serving: 246 calories, 5 g protein, 12 g carbohydrates, 21 g total fat, 10 mg cholesterol, 151 mg sodium*

## Parsley Potato Salad

*Preparation time: About 20 minutes*

*Cooking time: About 30 minutes*

*Chilling time: 2 to 3 hours*

Classic in its simplicity, this salad derives its flavor from generous amounts of parsley and onion.

- 4 **pounds medium-size thin-skinned potatoes**
    **Onion Cream Dressing (recipe follows)**
- 1 **cup finely chopped parsley**
    **Salt**

In a 5- to 6-quart pan, bring 3 quarts water to a boil over high heat. Add potatoes; reduce heat to medium, cover, and cook until tender when pierced (25 to 30 minutes). Meanwhile, prepare Onion Cream Dressing and set aside.

Drain potatoes; let cool. Peel, if desired, and cut into ¼-inch-thick slices; place in a bowl. Add dressing and all but 2 tablespoons of the parsley. Mix gently. Season to taste with salt. Cover and refrigerate for 2 to 3 hours. Garnish with reserved parsley. Transport in a cooler. Makes 10 to 12 servings.

***Onion Cream Dressing.*** Mix 1 cup *each* **sour cream** and **mayonnaise,** 6 tablespoons **white wine vinegar,** and 1 large **onion,** finely chopped.

*Per serving: 299 calories, 4 g protein, 30 g carbohydrates, 19 g total fat, 19 mg cholesterol, 126 mg sodium*

# Breads for Non-bakers

*It's almost a joke among potluck planners that those who don't like to cook can always be asked to bring bread—usually a loaf purchased on the way to the party. If you find yourself relegated to the "bread" category, take heart. Get ready to surprise everyone with home-baked goodness. Using a food processor to mix and knead the dough simplifies bread-making so much that even the inexperienced can easily turn out a lovely loaf.*

## Herb Bread

1 package active dry yeast
1 teaspoon sugar
¾ cup warm water (about 100°F)
2 tablespoons salad oil
    About 2¾ cups all-purpose flour
½ cup cornmeal
2 tablespoons toasted instant minced onion
1 teaspoon *each* celery seeds and salt
¾ teaspoon *each* rubbed sage and dry rosemary
¼ teaspoon pepper
1 egg

Stir together yeast, sugar, and water; let stand until foamy (8 to 10 minutes). Stir in oil.

In a food processor fitted with a metal blade, combine 2½ cups of the flour, cornmeal, onion, celery seeds, salt, sage, rosemary, and pepper; process just until blended. Add egg. With machine running, pour in yeast mixture in a slow, steady stream.

Run machine for 45 seconds to knead dough. It should be slightly sticky; if too wet, add some of the remaining flour, a tablespoon at a time.

Remove dough and shape into a ball. Turn ball over in greased bowl, cover with plastic wrap, and let rise in a warm place until doubled (about 1½ hours).

Punch down dough and knead briefly on a floured board, shaping into a smooth loaf. Place in a greased 4½- by 8½-inch loaf pan. Cover lightly with plastic wrap; let stand until loaf has risen about 1¼ inches above pan rim (about 45 minutes). Discard plastic.

Bake in a 375° oven until well browned (about 35 minutes). Turn out of pan onto a rack to cool. Makes 1 loaf (about 16 slices).

*Per slice: 118 calories, 3 g protein, 21 g carbohydrates, 2 g total fat, 17 mg cholesterol, 143 mg sodium*

## Whole Wheat Country Loaf
*Pictured on page 83*

Follow directions for **Herb Bread** but omit cornmeal, toasted onion, celery seeds, sage, rosemary, pepper, and egg. Increase warm water to 1 cup; decrease salad oil to 1 tablespoon. After yeast is foamy, stir in 2 tablespoons **molasses** with oil.

Instead of 2¾ cups all-purpose flour, use 1¼ cups **whole wheat flour** and 1½ cups **all-purpose flour.** To flour mixture add ¼ cup **wheat germ.** Add up to ¼ cup more all-purpose flour if dough is too wet after processing. Decrease first rising time to between 50 minutes and 1¼ hours.

When dough has risen, shape into a smooth 10-inch-long cylinder and place on a greased baking sheet. Decrease rising time to between 20 and 35 minutes. Before baking, brush lightly with a mixture of 1 **egg white** and 2 teaspoons **water;** cut three ½-inch-deep diagonal slashes in top of loaf.

Bake until loaf is well browned and sounds hollow when tapped (30 to 35 minutes).

## Parmesan Cheese Bread
*Pictured on page 46*

Follow directions for **Herb Bread** but omit cornmeal, toasted onion, celery seeds, sage, rosemary, and pepper. Instead of salad oil, use 2 tablespoons **olive oil.** Instead of 2¾ cups all-purpose flour, use 1 cup **whole wheat flour** and about 1½ cups **all-purpose flour.** Decrease salt to ½ teaspoon. Add ½ cup **whole-bran cereal** and 1¼ cups (about 5 oz.) **freshly grated Parmesan cheese** to flour mixture in processor.

When dough has risen, shape into a smooth ball and place on a greased baking sheet. Sprinkle with ¼ cup more grated Parmesan cheese before baking. Decrease baking time to between 30 and 35 minutes.

**Potluck Classics**

*An updated version of the traditional potluck favorites—potato salad, fried chicken, and pie—features (clockwise from bottom) Sweet Onion Potato Salad (facing page), Parmesan Dijon Chicken (page 63), and Glazed Berry Tarts (page 92). Fresh asparagus spears round out the menu.*

# Sweet Onion Potato Salad

*Pictured on facing page*

*Pictured on facing page*

Preparation time: *About 20 minutes*

Cooking time: *About 30 minutes*

Chilling time: *At least 2 hours*

Sweet onion, apple, pickles, and stuffed green olives elevate this generous-size potato salad to new heights. It can be made as much as a day ahead of the potluck.

- **3 pounds medium-size red thin-skinned potatoes**
- **1 large Walla Walla onion or other mild red or white onion**
- **1 cup thinly sliced celery**
- **1 large Golden Delicious apple (unpeeled), cored and diced**
- **12 pimento-stuffed green olives, sliced**
- **⅓ cup chopped sweet pickles**
- **1½ cups mayonnaise**
- **1 teaspoon Dijon mustard**
- **2 tablespoons distilled white vinegar**
- **1 teaspoon bottled steak sauce or soy sauce**
  **Salt and pepper**
  **Pickle strips (optional)**

In a 4- to 5-quart pan, bring 2 quarts water to a boil over high heat. Add potatoes; reduce heat to medium, cover, and cook until tender when pierced (25 to 30 minutes). Drain and let cool. Peel potatoes, if desired, and dice; place in a large bowl.

Cut onion into quarters and slice thinly; add to potatoes along with celery, apple, olives, and chopped pickles.

In a small bowl, stir together mayonnaise, mustard, vinegar, and steak sauce. Spoon over potato mixture and mix gently. Season to taste with salt and pepper. Cover and refrigerate for at least 2 hours or for up to a day. Garnish with pickle strips, if desired. Transport in a cooler. Makes 10 to 12 servings.

*Per serving: 315 calories, 3 g protein, 27 g carbohydrates, 22 g total fat, 16 mg cholesterol, 311 mg sodium*

# Potato & Vegetable Salad

Preparation time: *About 30 minutes*

Cooking time: *About 40 minutes*

Colorful vegetables and a tangy yogurt dressing lighten that grand potluck standby, potato salad. Set it out as soon as it's ready or refrigerate it for an hour or two before serving.

- **6 medium-size russet or thin-skinned potatoes (about 2 lbs. *total*)**
- **1 medium-size zucchini**
- **2 medium-size carrots**
- **½ pound green beans**
  **Yogurt Dressing (recipe follows)**
  **Salt and pepper**

In a 6- to 8-quart pan, bring 4 quarts water to a boil over high heat. Add potatoes; reduce heat to medium, cover, and cook until tender when pierced (25 to 30 minutes). Drain and let cool.

Meanwhile, slice zucchini and carrots ¼ inch thick. Cut beans into 1½-inch lengths.

In same pan, bring 2 to 3 quarts water to a boil. Add zucchini and cook, uncovered, until tender-crisp to bite (about 2 minutes). Lift zucchini out with a slotted spoon and immerse in cold water. Add carrots to boiling water and cook until tender-crisp to bite (about 5 minutes). Lift carrots out with a slotted spoon and add to water with zucchini. Add beans to boiling water and cook until tender-crisp to bite (about 6 minutes). Drain beans and add to zucchini and carrots. Drain cooled vegetables well and transfer to a large bowl.

Meanwhile, prepare Yogurt Dressing and set aside.

Peel potatoes and dice into ½-inch cubes; add to vegetables. Pour dressing over vegetables and mix lightly. Season to taste with salt and pepper. (At this point, you may cover and refrigerate for up to 2 hours.) Transport in a cooler. Makes 6 to 8 servings.

***Yogurt Dressing.*** Combine ⅓ cup *each* **plain yogurt** and **mayonnaise,** ½ cup finely chopped **onion,** 2 tablespoons finely chopped **parsley,** and 1 tablespoon **lemon juice.** Mix until well blended.

*Per serving: 184 calories, 4 g protein, 27 g carbohydrates, 8 g total fat, 6 mg cholesterol, 75 mg sodium*

## Crunchy Vegetable & Bulgur Salad

*Pictured on page 27*

*Preparation time: 1¼ hours*

*Chilling time: At least 4 hours*

Crisp vegetables contrast agreeably with chewy bulgur in this salad. Make it ahead so the flavors of the dressing will be thoroughly absorbed.

  1  **cup** *each* **bulgur wheat and water**
     **Lemon-Basil Dressing (recipe follows)**
  2  **medium-size carrots, thinly sliced**
  ½  **cup thinly sliced green onions (including tops)**
  1  **small green bell pepper, seeded and finely chopped**
  1  **stalk celery, thinly sliced**
     **Romaine lettuce leaves, washed and crisped**
  1  **or 2 medium-size tomatoes, cut into wedges**
  2  **ounces alfalfa sprouts (optional)**

In a large bowl, combine bulgur and water; let stand for 1 hour. Meanwhile, prepare Lemon-Basil Dressing and set aside.

Drain bulgur well. Add carrots, green onions, bell pepper, celery, and dressing; mix well. Cover and refrigerate, stirring occasionally, for at least 4 hours or for up to a day. Line a bowl or platter with lettuce and fill with bulgur mixture. Garnish with tomatoes and, if desired, alfalfa sprouts. Transport in a cooler. Makes 6 to 8 servings.

***Lemon-Basil Dressing.*** Combine ¼ cup **lemon juice;** ⅓ cup **salad oil** or olive oil; 2 cloves **garlic,** minced or pressed; 1 teaspoon **salt;** 1½ teaspoons **dry basil;** ½ teaspoon *each* **dry mustard** and **sugar;** and ¼ teaspoon **pepper.** Mix until well blended.

*Per serving: 179 calories, 3 g protein, 22 g carbohydrates, 9 g total fat, 0 mg cholesterol, 290 mg sodium*

## Mixed Rice Salad

*Preparation time: About 1 hour*

*Cooking time: 30 minutes*

Colorful crisp vegetables are combined with hearty, seasoned long-grain and wild rice in this popular potluck offering.

  2¼  **cups water**
  1  **package (6 oz.) long-grain and wild rice mix**
  ½  **cup** *each* **mayonnaise, plain yogurt, and thinly sliced green onions (including tops)**
  ¼  **cup finely chopped parsley**
     **Salt and pepper**
  1  **cup** *each* **diced peeled cucumbers and tomatoes**
  ¼  **to ½ cup finely chopped celery**
  ½  **cup frozen peas, thawed**

In a 2- to 3-quart pan, bring water to a boil over high heat. Add rice and return to a boil. (Do not use seasoning packet; if seasoning is mixed with rice, rinse rice before cooking to remove seasoning.) Reduce heat, cover, and simmer until water is absorbed and rice is tender (about 30 minutes). Let stand at room temperature, uncovered, until cool (about 45 minutes).

Fluff rice with a fork; then stir in mayonnaise, yogurt, green onions, and parsley. Season to taste with salt and pepper. Transfer mixture to a salad bowl. Layer cucumbers, tomatoes, celery, and peas over rice. (At this point, you may cover and refrigerate for up to 4 hours.) Transport in a cooler. Mix lightly just before serving. Makes 6 servings.

*Per serving: 262 calories, 6 g protein, 27 g carbohydrates, 15 g total fat, 12 mg cholesterol, 561 mg sodium*

## Guacamole Pasta Salad

*Preparation time: 30 minutes*

*Cooking time: 15 minutes*

Present this colorful vegetable-pasta salad at a summer picnic potluck. The mellow avocado dressing, preserved by a generous drizzling of lemon juice, stays green for up to an hour.

  2  **cups (6 oz.) mixed colors dry spiral-shape pasta**
  1  **pound green beans, cut into 1-inch lengths**
  1  **medium-size carrot, coarsely shredded**
  ½  **cup thinly sliced green onions (including tops)**
  2  **tablespoons salad oil**
  6  **tablespoons lemon juice**
  2  **large softly ripe avocados**
     **Red lettuce leaves, washed and crisped**
     **Salt and pepper**

In a 5- to 6-quart pan, cook pasta in 3 quarts boiling water just until tender to bite (10 to 12 minutes). Or cook according to package directions. Drain, rinse with cold water, and drain well again.

Meanwhile, in a 2- to 3-quart pan, bring ½ inch water to a boil over high heat. Add beans, cover, and boil gently until tender-crisp to bite (about 5 minutes). Drain and let cool.

In a large bowl, combine pasta, beans, carrot, green onions, oil, and 2 tablespoons of the lemon juice; mix lightly. (At this point, you may cover and refrigerate for up to 4 hours.)

Up to 1 hour before serving, pit, peel, and mash avocados with remaining 4 tablespoons lemon juice. Arrange pasta mixture in a large salad bowl. Tuck lettuce around salad. Spoon avocado mixture over salad. Transport in a cooler. Offer salt and pepper to add to taste. Makes 8 servings.

*Per serving: 235 calories, 5 g protein, 27 g carbohydrates, 13 g total fat, 0 mg cholesterol, 16 mg sodium*

## Sweet Corn Coblets

*Pictured on page 75*

■ ■

*Preparation time: 10 minutes*

*Cooking time: 5 minutes*

When you expect kids, tempt them with these sweet-tart wheels of corn. Served at room temperature, they make great nibbling for all ages.

- **6 medium-size ears corn, cut into ¾-inch-thick rounds**
- **¾ cup distilled white vinegar**
- **1 cup finely chopped onion**
- **2 to 3 tablespoons sugar**
- **1 jar (2 oz.) chopped pimentos, drained**
- **1 teaspoon *each* mustard seeds and crushed red pepper**
- **½ teaspoon salt**

In a 6- to 8-quart pan, bring 4 quarts water to a boil over high heat. Add corn; cover and cook until hot (2 to 3 minutes). Drain and arrange in a 9- by 13-inch dish or rimmed serving platter.

In same pan, combine vinegar, onion, sugar, pimentos, mustard seeds, red pepper, and salt. Bring to a boil over high heat and cook, stirring, until sugar is dissolved. Pour over corn; let stand until cool, spooning mixture over corn frequently. If made ahead, cover and refrigerate for up to 6 hours. Serve at room temperature as finger food. Makes 8 to 10 servings.

*Per serving: 70 calories, 2 g protein, 16 g carbohydrates, .82 g total fat, 0 mg cholesterol, 120 mg sodium*

## High Desert Corn Casserole

■ ■

*Preparation time: 35 minutes*

*Baking time: About 30 minutes*

Fresh corn and piquant chiles stand out in this creamy, cheese-topped casserole. Bring it along to a summer potluck to complement barbecued chicken or steak.

- **4 to 5 large ears corn**
- **5 fresh jalapeño or serrano chiles**
- **2 tablespoons salad oil**
- **1 medium-size onion, chopped**
- **1 medium-size red bell pepper, seeded and finely chopped**
- **1 cup small curd cottage cheese**
- **2 eggs**
- **1 tablespoon cornstarch**
   **Salt and pepper**
- **1 cup (4 oz.) shredded Cheddar cheese**

Cut corn kernels from cobs to make 4 cups; set aside. Seed and finely chop 3 of the chiles. Heat oil in a wide frying pan over medium-high heat. Add chopped chiles, onion, and bell pepper. Cook, stirring often, until onion is limp and pepper is tender to bite (3 to 5 minutes). Add 2 cups of the corn and stir until hot.

Meanwhile, in a food processor or blender, combine remaining 2 cups corn, cottage cheese, eggs, and cornstarch. Whirl until smoothly puréed.

Remove cooked vegetables from heat and stir in puréed corn mixture. Season to taste with salt and pepper. Spread mixture in a lightly greased shallow 10-inch round or oval baking dish. Sprinkle with Cheddar cheese. (At this point, you may cover and refrigerate for up to 8 hours.) Transport in a cooler.

Bake, uncovered, in a 375° oven until mixture puffs in center and cheese begins to brown at edges (about 30 minutes). Garnish with remaining whole chiles. Makes 8 servings.

*Per serving: 213 calories, 11 g protein, 19 g carbohydrates, 12 g total fat, 87 mg cholesterol, 224 mg sodium*

## Swiss Mushroom Spaghetti Squash

*Pictured on facing page*

◆◆

*Preparation time: 1 hour*

*Baking time: 15 to 20 minutes*

Golden strands of spaghetti squash make a flavorful hot vegetable side dish that's pleasingly light. Team it with roast turkey or beef—or with grilled steaks or sausages. If you cook the squash in a microwave, you'll cut preparation time down to about 30 minutes.

- 1 **spaghetti squash (about 2 lbs.)**
- 4 **slices bacon**
- ½ **pound mushrooms, thinly sliced**
- ¼ **teaspoon freshly grated or ground nutmeg**
- 2 **cups (8 oz.) shredded Swiss cheese**
  **Thinly sliced green onions (including tops)**

Place whole spaghetti squash in a shallow baking pan. Pierce in several places with a fork. Bake in a 350° oven until shell yields slightly when pressed (about 1 hour). Or, to cook in a microwave, pierce whole squash in several places with a fork. Place in oven on a paper towel. Microwave on HIGH (100%), turning squash over once or twice, for 15 to 20 minutes or until shell yields slightly when pressed.

Meanwhile, in a wide frying pan, cook bacon over medium heat until crisp. Lift out, drain, crumble, and set aside. Reserve drippings in pan. Add mushrooms to pan and cook, stirring, until lightly browned (about 5 minutes). Mix in nutmeg. Remove a few of the mushrooms and reserve for garnish.

Cut squash in half lengthwise. Scoop out and discard seeds. With a fork, pull strands of pulp from shell and add to mushrooms in pan; mix in cheese and bacon. Spread squash mixture in a shallow 2-quart baking dish; garnish with reserved mushrooms. (At this point, you may cover and refrigerate for up to 8 hours.) Transport casserole and green onions separately in a cooler.

Bake, uncovered, in a 350° oven just until cheese is melted and squash is hot (15 to 20 minutes). Sprinkle with green onions. Makes 6 servings.

*Per serving: 272 calories, 14 g protein, 10 g carbohydrates, 20 g total fat, 45 mg cholesterol, 222 mg sodium*

## Eggplant Monterey

◆◆

*Preparation time: 50 minutes*

*Baking time: 35 to 40 minutes*

California's counterpart to Italy's eggplant parmigiana bears a close resemblance. Abundant with cheese, it can serve as either a substantial side dish or a meatless entrée.

- 2 **medium-size eggplants (about 1 lb. *each*)**
- 3 **tablespoons butter or margarine**
- 3 **tablespoons olive oil**
- 2 **teaspoons Italian herb seasoning or ½ teaspoon *each* dry basil, oregano, thyme, and marjoram**
- ½ **pound mushrooms, thinly sliced**
- 1 **large can (15 oz.) tomato sauce**
- 4 **cups (1 lb.) shredded jack cheese**
- ½ **cup freshly grated Parmesan cheese**

Cut eggplants (unpeeled) crosswise into ½-inch-thick slices. Arrange in a single layer in 2 shallow rimmed baking pans.

In a 9- to 10-inch frying pan, combine butter, olive oil, and Italian herb seasoning; place over medium heat until butter is melted. Brush butter mixture sparingly over eggplant; reserve remaining butter mixture in pan.

Broil eggplant about 4 inches below heat until lightly browned (8 to 10 minutes); turn and brush with some of the remaining butter mixture. Return to broiler and broil until eggplant is browned and soft when pressed (8 to 10 more minutes).

Meanwhile, add mushrooms to remaining butter mixture in pan and cook over medium-high heat, stirring, until liquid has evaporated and mushrooms are lightly browned; set aside.

Spread a third of the tomato sauce in a 9- by 13-inch baking dish and layer with half the eggplant and half the mushrooms. Cover with another third of the tomato sauce and half the jack cheese. Sprinkle with half the Parmesan cheese. Repeat layers, using remaining eggplant, mushrooms, tomato sauce, and cheeses. (At this point, you may cover and refrigerate for up to a day.) Transport in a cooler.

Bake, covered, in a 400° oven for 20 minutes. Uncover and continue baking until sauce is bubbly and top is browned (15 to 20 more minutes). Makes 8 servings.

*Per serving: 376 calories, 19 g protein, 13 g carbohydrates, 29 g total fat, 66 mg cholesterol, 793 mg sodium*

**Harvest Sampler**

*Celebrate autumn's bounty with (clockwise from top right) robust Wine-simmered Beef Cubes (page 73), Swiss Mushroom Spaghetti Squash (facing page), and a dessert of Fruit Crisp made with fresh pears (page 92).*

# Green Beans Oriental

*Preparation time: 35 minutes*

*Baking time: 20 to 25 minutes*

With its bold red and green accents, this stir-fry of tender-crisp vegetables adds appetizing color to any potluck table. After stir-frying, you assemble the vegetables in a casserole and bake just before serving.

- ½ cup slivered almonds
- ¼ cup salad oil
- ½ pound mushrooms, thinly sliced
- 1 package (9 oz.) frozen Italian green beans
- 1 cup diagonally sliced celery
- 1 medium-size green bell pepper, seeded and cut diagonally into thin slivers
- 1 clove garlic, minced or pressed
- 1½ tablespoons cornstarch
- 1 cup regular-strength chicken broth
- ¾ teaspoon salt
- 1 jar (2 oz.) diced pimentos, drained
- 1 can (8 oz.) sliced water chestnuts, drained

Toast almonds in a wide frying pan over medium heat until golden (6 to 8 minutes), shaking pan often. Remove from pan and set aside.

Pour oil into same pan; increase heat to medium-high. When oil is hot, add mushrooms and cook, stirring, until lightly browned. Add beans, celery, and bell pepper; continue cooking and stirring until celery is tender-crisp (6 to 8 minutes). Stir in garlic and remove from heat.

With a slotted spoon, transfer vegetables to a shallow 1½-quart casserole; sprinkle with half the almonds. Discard oil from pan.

Off heat, add cornstarch to same pan; gradually blend in broth. Return to medium-high heat and cook, stirring constantly, until bubbly and thickened. Stir in salt, pimentos, and water chestnuts. Pour over vegetable mixture in casserole. (At this point, you may cover and refrigerate for up to 8 hours.)

Bake, covered, in a 350° oven until hot (20 to 25 minutes). Sprinkle with remaining almonds. Makes 6 to 8 servings.

*Per serving: 160 calories, 4 g protein, 12 g carbohydrates, 12 g total fat, 0 mg cholesterol, 352 mg sodium*

# Summer Squash Gratin

*Preparation time: About 1 hour*

*Baking time: About 1½ hours*

Reminiscent of ratatouille, this colorful baked vegetable dish combines eggplant, onion, and tomato with sliced summer squash and bell pepper rings. Balance its exuberance by serving it with simply cooked meat, poultry, or fish.

- 5 to 7 tablespoons olive oil or salad oil
- 2 large onions, thinly sliced
- 2 small eggplants (about 1½ lbs. *total*), cut into ½-inch cubes (unpeeled)
- ½ teaspoon ground sage
- ¾ teaspoon dry thyme
- 2 large tomatoes, chopped
  Salt and pepper
- 1½ pounds summer squash (zucchini, crookneck, or pattypan), sliced crosswise about ¼ inch thick
- ¾ to 1 pound small green, red, or yellow bell peppers, seeded and cut into ¼-inch rings
- ½ cup freshly grated Parmesan cheese

Pour 4 tablespoons of the oil into a wide frying pan over medium heat. Add onions, eggplants, sage, and ½ teaspoon of the thyme. Cook, stirring often, until liquid has evaporated, onions are pale gold, and eggplants begin to fall apart (about 40 minutes). Add up to 2 more tablespoons oil, if needed.

Add tomatoes, increase heat to high, and cook, stirring often, until liquid has evaporated. Season

to taste with salt and pepper. Spoon mixture into a shallow 2½- to 3-quart baking dish or pan.

Sprinkle squash slices lightly with salt, pepper, and remaining ¼ teaspoon thyme. Arrange squash slices and bell pepper rings in alternating rows on onion mixture, overlapping vegetables. Sprinkle with remaining 1 tablespoon oil. (At this point, you may cover and refrigerate for up to a day.)

Bake, uncovered, in a 350° oven until squash is tender when pierced (about 1¼ hours). Sprinkle with cheese and continue baking until cheese is melted and slightly browned (5 to 10 more minutes). Insulate to transport hot (see page 5). Makes 8 servings.

*Per serving: 183 calories, 6 g protein, 15 g carbohydrates, 12 g total fat, 5 mg cholesterol, 125 mg sodium*

## Layered Enchilada Casserole

*Preparation time: 35 minutes*

*Baking time: About 35 minutes*

This meatless version of enchiladas—layers of tortilla strips, tomato sauce, sour cream, and cheese—provides a colorful accent for a buffet of Mexican-style dishes.

> 1 tablespoon salad oil
> ¼ cup chopped onion
> 1 large can (28 oz.) tomatoes
> 2 cans (about 2 oz. *each*) sliced ripe olives, drained
> 1 can (4 oz.) diced green chiles
>   Salt
> 9 corn tortillas (6 inches in diameter), cut into 1-inch-wide strips
> 1½ cups sour cream
> 2 cups (8 oz.) shredded Cheddar cheese

Heat oil in a wide frying pan over medium-high heat. Add onion and cook, stirring often, until onion begins to brown (about 5 minutes). Add tomatoes (break up with a spoon) and their liquid, olives, and chiles. Increase heat to high and bring mixture to a boil; reduce heat and boil gently, uncovered, for 10 minutes. Remove from heat; season to taste with salt.

In a shallow 2-quart casserole, layer a third each of the tortilla strips, tomato sauce, sour cream, and cheese. Repeat two more times, ending with cheese. (At this point, you may cover and refrigerate for up to 3 hours.) Transport in a cooler.

Bake, uncovered, in a 350° oven until mixture is hot in center and bubbly at edges (about 35 minutes). Makes 6 to 8 servings.

*Per serving: 348 calories, 12 g protein, 23 g carbohydrates, 24 g total fat, 49 mg cholesterol, 613 mg sodium*

## Sweet & Sour Baked Beans

*Pictured on front cover*

*Preparation time: 35 minutes*

*Baking time: 1¼ to 1½ hours*

Four kinds of beans go into this colorful casserole. Tangy with old-fashioned flavor, the beans take little time to prepare because they're canned. Enjoy with barbecued steak, sausages, or chicken.

> ½ pound (about 10 slices) bacon (5 slices)
> 4 large onions, thinly sliced
> 1 cup firmly packed brown sugar
> 1½ teaspoons dry mustard
> ½ cup cider vinegar
> 2 cans (1 lb. *each*) dry butter beans (California limas)
> 1 can (15½ oz.) green lima beans
> 1 can (about 15 oz.) kidney beans
> 1 large can (28 oz.) New England–style baked beans

In a wide frying pan, cook bacon over medium heat until crisp. Lift out, drain, crumble, and set aside. Discard all but ¼ cup of the drippings. Add onions to drippings, separating onions into rings. Stir in brown sugar, mustard, and vinegar; cook over medium heat, stirring occasionally, until juices are reduced by half (about 10 minutes).

Drain butter beans, lima beans, and kidney beans. Combine with *undrained* baked beans in a 3- to 3½-quart casserole. Add onion-vinegar mixture and all but 2 tablespoons of the bacon; stir gently until blended. (At this point, you may cover and refrigerate for up to a day.)

Bake, covered, in a 350° oven until hot and bubbly (1¼ to 1½ hours). Garnish with reserved bacon. Insulate to transport hot (see page 5). Makes 10 to 12 servings.

*Per serving: 326 calories, 13 g protein, 56 g carbohydrates, 7 g total fat, 12 mg cholesterol, 859 mg sodium*

**Buon Appetito!**

*Crisp bread sticks, a selection of cold cuts, and other tempting tidbits from the
neighborhood deli accompany Three-color Vegetable Tetrazzini (facing page), an
Italian-inspired dish originally named for an opera star.*

## Three-color Vegetable Tetrazzini

*Pictured on facing page*

◼◼

*Preparation time: 45 minutes*

*Baking time: About 40 minutes*

Combining both pasta and vegetables in one dish, this versatile casserole mixes carrots, zucchini, and cauliflowerets with spinach noodles.

    6   tablespoons butter or margarine
    ½   cup all-purpose flour
    1   teaspoon salt
    ½   teaspoon *each* white pepper and ground nutmeg
    ½   teaspoon dry oregano
    1   can (14½ oz.) regular-strength chicken broth
    2   cups milk
    ¼   cup dry sherry or additional milk
    ⅔   cup grated Parmesan cheese
        About ¾ pound *each* cauliflower, carrots, and zucchini
    1   package (12 oz.) dry spinach noodles
    ⅓   cup sliced almonds

In a 2-quart pan, melt butter over medium heat. Stir in flour, salt, white pepper, nutmeg, and oregano. Cook, stirring, until bubbly. Remove from heat and gradually stir in broth and milk. Return to heat and cook, stirring constantly, until sauce boils and thickens. Remove from heat and stir in sherry and ⅓ cup of the cheese.

Cut cauliflower into bite-size flowerets. Slice carrots and zucchini diagonally ¼ inch thick. (You should have about 3 cups of each.) Place on a rack over 1 inch boiling water. Cover and steam until just tender when pierced (7 to 9 minutes).

Meanwhile, in a 4- to 5-quart pan, cook noodles in 3 quarts boiling water just until tender to bite (8 to 10 minutes). Or cook according to package directions. Drain well. In a bowl, lightly mix noodles and half the sauce. Spread in a shallow 3-quart baking dish. Top with vegetables and remaining sauce. (At this point, you may cover and refrigerate for up to 8 hours.) Transport casserole and remaining cheese separately in a cooler.

Bake, covered, in a 350° oven for 20 minutes; sprinkle with nuts and remaining ⅓ cup cheese. Continue baking, uncovered, until hot and bubbly (about 20 more minutes). Makes 8 to 10 servings.

*Per serving: 326 calories, 12 g protein, 39 g carbohydrates, 14 g total fat, 62 mg cholesterol, 617 mg sodium*

## Chard, Feta & Fila Pie

*Pictured on page 22*

◼◼

*Preparation time: 35 minutes*

*Baking time: 40 to 45 minutes*

A fine complement to roast leg of lamb or barbecued lamb chops, this fila-topped vegetable and cheese casserole can also be served as a meatless main dish with a tomato and cucumber salad.

    2   pounds Swiss chard, coarse stems removed
    5   tablespoons butter or margarine
    1   large onion, thinly sliced
    4   eggs
    1½  teaspoons *each* dry basil and oregano
    ¼   teaspoon pepper
    2   cups (about 12 oz.) crumbled feta cheese
    4   sheets (12 by 17 inches) fila dough

Fill a 5- to 6-quart pan three-quarters full of water and bring to a boil over high heat. Push about a third of the chard leaves at a time into water; cook, uncovered, until stems are limp (about 3 minutes). Lift out chard with a slotted spoon and drain. Repeat with remaining chard. Let cool; then chop coarsely.

Meanwhile, in a wide frying pan, melt 2 tablespoons of the butter over medium heat. Add onion and cook, stirring occasionally, until soft (about 10 minutes).

In a large bowl, beat eggs just until blended. Stir in chard, onion, basil, oregano, pepper, and feta. Spread mixture in a shallow 2-quart baking dish or pan.

Stack sheets of fila and fold once so width fits or is slightly larger than narrow dimension of baking dish. Set baking dish on fila; cut around dish so fila will fit, discarding trimmings.

Melt remaining 3 tablespoons butter. Lay a sheet of fila on chard mixture; brush with butter. Layer remaining fila, brushing each layer with remaining butter. With a sharp knife, cut through fila, making about 6 equal-size diamonds. (At this point, you may cover and refrigerate for up to a day.)

Bake, uncovered, in a 375° oven until fila is well browned (40 to 45 minutes). Insulate to transport hot (see page 5). Cut through markings to serve. Makes 6 servings.

*Per serving: 375 calories, 17 g protein, 21 g carbohydrates, 26 g total fat, 259 mg cholesterol, 1074 mg sodium*

## Zucchini Jack Casserole

Preparation time: 25 minutes

Baking time: 35 to 40 minutes

Overloaded with zucchini from your garden? Season the zucchini with garlic, green chiles, and onion, and then bake in a cheese custard to serve with fried or barbecued chicken.

2 pounds (about 8 small) zucchini
4 eggs
½ cup milk
1 teaspoon salt
2 teaspoons baking powder
3 tablespoons all-purpose flour
¼ cup chopped parsley
1 clove garlic, minced or pressed
1 small onion, finely chopped
1 large can (7 oz.) diced green chiles
3 cups (12 oz.) shredded jack cheese
1 cup seasoned croutons
3 tablespoons butter or margarine, melted

Slice zucchini ¼ inch thick (you should have about 7 cups). In a large bowl, beat together eggs, milk, salt, baking powder, and flour until smooth. Stir in parsley, garlic, onion, chiles, cheese, and zucchini. Spoon into a greased 9- by 13-inch baking dish. Lightly mix croutons with melted butter; sprinkle over zucchini mixture. (At this point, you may cover and refrigerate for up to 3 hours.) Transport in a cooler.

Bake, uncovered, in a 350° oven until mixture is set in center and zucchini is tender when pierced (35 to 40 minutes). Let stand for about 10 minutes before cutting. Makes about 10 servings.

*Per serving: 246 calories, 13 g protein, 10 g carbohydrates, 17 g total fat, 150 mg cholesterol, 750 mg sodium*

## Layered Spinach Casserole

Preparation time: 45 minutes

Baking time: About 25 minutes

Here's hearty vegetarian nourishment in an egg and spinach casserole suitable as either a side dish or an entrée.

2 cups water
1 cup long-grain brown rice
¾ pound spinach
4 eggs
¼ teaspoon *each* celery seeds, dry oregano, and pepper
2 tablespoons soy sauce
2 tablespoons finely chopped parsley
1½ cups (6 oz.) shredded Cheddar cheese
¼ cup butter or margarine, melted
¾ cup toasted wheat germ

In a 1½- to 2-quart pan, bring water to a boil over high heat. Add rice; reduce heat, cover, and simmer until tender to bite (about 35 minutes).

Meanwhile, discard coarse spinach leaves and stems. Rinse remaining leaves well, pat dry, and chop finely. In a large bowl, beat eggs with celery seeds, oregano, pepper, 1 tablespoon of the soy sauce, and parsley; stir in spinach.

Mix cheese into rice and pat mixture evenly into a greased 10-inch quiche dish or pie plate. Fill with spinach mixture. In a small bowl, stir together butter, wheat germ, and remaining 1 tablespoon soy sauce; pat evenly over spinach. (At this point, you may cover and refrigerate for up to 8 hours.) Transport in a cooler.

Bake, uncovered, in a 325° oven until spinach topping feels set when lightly pressed (about 25 minutes). Cut into wedges to serve. Makes 6 servings.

*Per serving: 413 calories, 19 g protein, 34 g carbohydrates, 23 g total fat, 233 mg cholesterol, 679 mg sodium*

## Potato-Cheese Casserole

Preparation time: 45 minutes

Baking time: 35 to 45 minutes

Lightly puffed and studded with sautéed mushrooms, this mashed potato casserole is gilded with Swiss cheese and sprinkled with crisp bacon.

4 large russet potatoes (about 2 lbs. *total*), peeled and quartered
5 tablespoons butter or margarine
½ pound mushrooms, sliced
1 clove garlic, minced or pressed
½ cup chopped parsley
2 eggs
2 cups (8 oz.) shredded Swiss cheese

¼ teaspoon salt
⅛ teaspoon *each* white pepper and ground nutmeg
2 or 3 slices bacon, crisply cooked and crumbled

In a 3-quart pan, bring 6 cups water to a boil over high heat. Add potatoes, cover, and boil gently until tender (20 to 30 minutes); drain well.

Meanwhile, in a wide frying pan, melt 2 tablespoons of the butter over medium-high heat. Add mushrooms and cook, stirring often, until liquid has evaporated. Stir in garlic and parsley; set aside.

In the large bowl of an electric mixer, beat potatoes until fluffy. Beat in remaining 3 tablespoons butter, eggs, 1½ cups of the cheese, salt, white pepper, and nutmeg. Stir in mushroom mixture. Spread in a greased shallow 1½- to 2-quart casserole. (At this point, you may cover and refrigerate for up to 8 hours.) Transport casserole, bacon, and remaining cheese separately in a cooler.

Bake, loosely covered, in a 400° oven until hot (25 to 30 minutes). Sprinkle with bacon and remaining ½ cup cheese. Continue baking, uncovered, until cheese is melted and lightly browned (10 to 15 more minutes). Makes 6 to 8 servings.

*Per serving: 278 calories, 13 g protein, 18 g carbohydrates, 18 g total fat, 116 mg cholesterol, 271 mg sodium*

# Green Onion–Rice Casserole

*Preparation time: 10 minutes*

*Baking time: 35 to 45 minutes*

Green onions lend color and flavor to this rice casserole; sour cream and cottage cheese give it a rich, creamy consistency.

1½ cups sliced green onions (including tops)
2 cups small curd cottage cheese
1 cup sour cream
¼ cup milk
2 cloves garlic, minced or pressed
1 teaspoon Worcestershire
3 cups cooked long-grain white rice
½ cup grated Parmesan cheese
¼ teaspoon liquid hot pepper seasoning (optional)
3 green onions, ends and tops trimmed

In a bowl, combine sliced green onions, cottage cheese, sour cream, milk, garlic, Worcestershire, rice, ¼ cup of the cheese, and, if desired, hot pep-

per seasoning; mix until well blended. Spoon mixture into a greased shallow 2-quart casserole; sprinkle with remaining ¼ cup cheese. (At this point, you may cover and refrigerate for up to a day.) Transport casserole and whole green onions separately in a cooler.

Bake, uncovered, in a 350° oven until hot and bubbly (35 to 45 minutes). Garnish with green onions. Makes 6 servings.

*Per serving: 313 calories, 16 g protein, 32 g carbohydrates, 14 g total fat, 34 mg cholesterol, 444 mg sodium*

# *Bulgur & Rice Pilaf*
*Pictured on page 22*

*Preparation time: 10 minutes*

*Cooking time: About 1¼ hours*

Mildly seasoned, this two-grain pilaf makes a satisfying accompaniment to either meat or poultry.

2 cups regular-strength chicken broth
½ cup bulgur wheat
3 tablespoons butter or margarine
1 small onion, finely chopped
1 stalk celery, finely chopped
¼ cup lightly packed chopped celery leaves
¼ teaspoon pepper
½ cup brown rice
1 large bay leaf
Whole celery leaves

In a 1- to 2-quart pan, bring 1 cup of the broth to a boil. Remove from heat; add bulgur. Cover and set aside until broth is absorbed (about 1 hour).

Meanwhile, in a 3- to 4-quart pan, melt butter over medium-high heat. Add onion, celery, chopped celery leaves, and pepper. Cook, stirring often, until onion is soft but not browned (about 8 minutes). Add rice and cook, stirring, until opaque (3 to 5 more minutes). Mix in bay leaf and remaining 1 cup broth. Increase heat to high and bring mixture to a boil; reduce heat, cover, and simmer until all liquid is absorbed (about 1 hour).

Lightly mix bulgur into rice mixture and transfer to a warm serving dish. Insulate to transport hot (see page 5). Garnish with whole celery leaves. Makes 6 servings.

*Per serving: 175 calories, 3 g protein, 25 g carbohydrates, 7 g total fat, 16 mg cholesterol, 406 mg sodium*

# Fish & Shellfish

Seafood's delicacy accounts for its popularity as an entrée, but it's that very same delicacy that challenges the potluck cook. How can seafood's just-cooked freshness be assured between kitchen and buffet table? One way, especially appealing in warm weather, is to serve poached fish cold in a salad, or blanketed with an exquisite sauce. For chillier times of year, try a savory chowder that both travels well and pleases guests. Tuna and other firm-textured fish, as well as such shellfish as scallops and clams, combine sumptuously in casseroles with potatoes or pasta.

## Veracruz Fish Salad

*Pictured on facing page*

*Preparation time: 40 minutes*

*Chilling time: At least 2 hours*

Refreshingly light and colorful, this fish salad brings a taste of the Mexican Gulf Coast to a summertime buffet table.

2½ **pounds white-fleshed fish fillets, such as rockfish or orange roughy**
3 **large tomatoes, coarsely diced**
⅔ **cup lime juice**
3 **cloves garlic, minced or pressed**
1 **cup sliced pimento-stuffed green olives**
⅓ **cup drained capers**
½ **cup thinly sliced green onions (including tops)**
  **Salt and pepper**
  **About 8 large iceberg lettuce leaves, washed and crisped**
1 **or 2 limes, cut into wedges**

Place fish in a 9- by 13-inch baking dish, overlapping fillets slightly. Cover and bake in a 400° oven just until opaque throughout when cut (12 to 15 minutes). Let cool; then cover and refrigerate for at least 2 hours or for up to a day.

Lift out fish, discarding pan juices. Pull out and discard any bones from fish. Break fish into bite-size chunks. In a large bowl, combine tomatoes, lime juice, garlic, olives, capers, green onions, and fish; mix gently. Season to taste with salt and pepper. Line a serving bowl with lettuce and spoon in salad. Garnish with lime wedges. Transport in a cooler. Makes 6 to 8 servings.

*Per serving: 179 calories, 28 g protein, 7 g carbohydrates, 5 g total fat, 50 mg cholesterol, 648 mg sodium*

### A Latin Fiesta

*Cool seafood specialties with Latin flavor and color include Veracruz Fish Salad
(facing page), at left, and Chile, Shrimp & Corn Salad (page 47), upper right.
Round out the menu with a platter of crisp tortilla chips and red salsa for dipping.*

# Sashimi Tray Salad

◼◼

*Preparation time: About 35 minutes*

*Chilling time: About 30 minutes*

Fresh sea bass or tuna, thinly sliced and marinated in a sesame-soy dressing, stars in this sashimi-style salad. Alongside are pickled ginger, green onions, cucumber, and bean sprouts—all to be dipped into a mixture of fiery wasabi paste and soy sauce.

> Soy-Sesame Dressing (recipe follows)
> 2 **pounds very fresh white sea bass fillets, or tuna fillets or steaks (*each* ¾ to 1 inch thick)**
> 1 **pound bean sprouts**
> 1 **European-style cucumber (8 to 10 inches long)**
> 10 **to 12 green onions (including tops), cut into thin diagonal slices**
> ½ **cup drained sliced pickled ginger**
> **About 1½ tablespoons wasabi paste or prepared horseradish**
> **About ½ cup soy sauce**

Prepare Soy-Sesame Dressing; set aside.

Thinly slice fish across grain. Lay slices in a single layer in a 9- by 13-inch baking dish and drizzle with half the dressing. Cover and refrigerate for about 30 minutes.

Meanwhile, in a medium-size bowl, combine bean sprouts with remaining dressing. Cover and refrigerate for about 30 minutes.

With tines of a fork, score cucumber lengthwise; then thinly slice. Transport fish, bean sprouts, cucumber, and green onions separately in a cooler.

To serve, arrange cucumber slices in center of a large platter. Lift fish from dressing with a slotted spoon and place to one side of cucumbers. Lift bean sprouts from dressing with a slotted spoon and arrange on other side of cucumbers; discard dressing. Garnish with green onions and ginger.

For dipping, let each guest spoon a little wasabi paste into a small dish and stir in about 1 tablespoon of the soy sauce. Makes 8 servings.

*Soy-Sesame Dressing.* Stir together ¾ cup **rice wine vinegar,** 3 tablespoons **soy sauce,** and ½ teaspoon **sesame oil.**

*Per serving: 155 calories, 24 g protein, 9 g carbohydrates, 3 g total fat, 47 mg cholesterol, 1246 mg sodium*

# Sole Fillets with Four-color Vegetable Salad

◼◼

*Preparation time: 1¼ hours*

*Cooking time: 15 minutes*

Cool poached sole rolls crown a colorful medley of crisp vegetables in a Szechwan peppercorn dressing. More than just a salad, it's a spectacular centerpiece for a summer potluck party.

> 3 **pounds small sole fillets (*each* about ¼ inch thick)**
> ½ **pound Chinese pea pods (also called snow or sugar peas)**
> **Szechwan Peppercorn Dressing (recipe follows)**
> 4 **medium-size red bell peppers, seeded and chopped**
> ½ **pound daikon, peeled and finely shredded**
> 4 *each* **small yellow crookneck squash and zucchini (about 2 lbs. *total*), cut into matchstick pieces**
> 6 **medium-size carrots, cut into thin diagonal slices**

Cut fillets in half lengthwise; roll each piece and thread onto an 8- to 10-inch skewer (use 8 skewers, placing about 6 rolls on each).

In a wide 6- to 8-quart pan, bring 5 quarts water to a boil over high heat. Lay skewered fish in water, cover, and immediately remove from heat. Let stand until fish is opaque throughout when cut (about 5 minutes). Lift skewers from water and lay flat in a dish; set aside.

Return water to a boil. Add pea pods and cook just until water returns to a boil. Drain quickly, immerse in cold water until cool, and drain again.

Prepare Szechwan Peppercorn Dressing. In a large bowl, combine bell peppers, daikon, squash, zucchini, carrots, and dressing; mix gently. (At this point, you may cover and refrigerate fish, pea pods, and vegetable mixture separately for up to a day.) Transport in a cooler.

To serve, lift out vegetable mixture with a slotted spoon, reserving dressing, and spread on a large, deep platter. Remove fish rolls from skewers and arrange over vegetables. Place pea pods around edge of platter. Spoon reserved dressing over fish and pea pods. Makes 8 to 12 servings.

*Szechwan Peppercorn Dressing.* Combine ¾ cup **rice wine vinegar** or white wine vinegar, ½ cup salad oil, 3 tablespoons soy sauce, 1½ tablespoons minced fresh ginger, 2 teaspoons Szechwan peppercorns, and ½ teaspoon chili oil or liquid hot pepper seasoning. Mix until well blended.

*Per serving: 234 calories, 24 g protein, 11 g carbohydrates, 11 g total fat, 54 mg cholesterol, 376 mg sodium*

# Layered Niçoise Salad

*Preparation time: 45 minutes*

*Cooking time: 30 minutes*

Not every salad can hold its own for a fair-weather potluck, but this one can. Layering keeps the butter lettuce crisp and attractive for up to a day.

> 1½  **pounds small thin-skinned potatoes (***each*** about 1½ inches in diameter)**
> **Anchovy Dressing (recipe follows)**
> **Salt and pepper**
> 1  **pound green beans, cut into 1-inch lengths**
> ¼  **cup** *each* **mayonnaise and sour cream**
> 1  **large can (12½ oz.) chunk-style tuna, drained**
> 5  **hard-cooked eggs, thinly sliced**
> 2  **quarts lightly packed bite-size pieces washed, crisped butter lettuce**

Place potatoes on a rack over about 1 inch boiling water. Cover and steam until tender when pierced (about 20 minutes).

Meanwhile, prepare Anchovy Dressing and set aside.

When potatoes are cool enough to touch, peel, if desired, and slice ¼ inch thick. Place in a deep 4- to 5-quart serving bowl. Add dressing and mix lightly; season to taste with salt and pepper. Let cool.

Meanwhile, place beans on a rack over about 1 inch boiling water. Cover and steam until bright green and tender to bite (about 10 minutes). Immerse in cold water until cool; then drain and pat dry.

Add mayonnaise and sour cream to potatoes; mix lightly. Layer beans over potatoes. With a fork, break tuna into bite-size pieces and distribute evenly over beans. Top with egg slices and then cover with lettuce. (At this point, you may cover and refrigerate for up to a day.) Transport in a cooler.

Just before serving, mix lightly. Makes 6 to 8 servings.

*Anchovy Dressing.* Combine ¾ cup **salad oil;** ½ cup *each* **lemon juice** and finely chopped **parsley;** 1 small **red onion,** finely chopped; ¼ cup **Dijon mustard;** 1 tablespoon drained **capers;** 4 canned **anchovy fillets,** minced; 1 large clove **garlic,** minced or pressed; and ¼ teaspoon **dill weed.** Mix until well blended.

*Per serving: 464 calories, 21 g protein, 25 g carbohydrates, 32 g total fat, 198 mg cholesterol, 578 mg sodium*

# Basil & Scallop Pasta Salad

*Preparation time: 45 minutes*

*Chilling time: At least 2 hours*

Broccoli, pasta, and scallops mingle delectably in this main-dish salad. To accentuate the seafood theme, you can use small seashell-shaped pasta.

> 8  **ounces twisted egg noodles**
> 4  **cups broccoli flowerets, cut into bite-size pieces**
> 1  **pound scallops, sliced ¼ inch thick**
> ¼  **cup** *each* **lemon juice and white wine vinegar**
> ½  **cup** *each* **olive oil and salad oil**
> 1  **teaspoon** *each* **dry mustard and sugar**
> 1  **clove garlic, minced or pressed**
> 1  **cup finely chopped fresh basil leaves**
> **Salt and pepper**

In a 6- to 8-quart pan, cook pasta in 4 quarts boiling water just until tender to bite (about 8 minutes). Or cook according to package directions. Drain, rinse with cold water, and drain again.

In a wide frying pan, bring ¼ inch water to a boil over high heat; add broccoli, cover, and cook just until tender-crisp (about 2 minutes). Drain and immerse in cold water until cool. Meanwhile, in same pan, bring another ¼ inch water to a gentle boil over medium-high heat. Add scallops, cover, and cook just until opaque throughout when cut (about 3 minutes). Drain both broccoli and scallops; set aside.

In a large bowl, combine lemon juice, vinegar, olive oil, salad oil, mustard, sugar, garlic, and basil; mix well. Add pasta, broccoli, and scallops; mix gently. Season to taste with salt and pepper. Cover and refrigerate for at least 2 hours or for up to a day. Transport in a cooler. Makes 6 servings.

*Per serving: 578 calories, 21 g protein, 38 g carbohydrates, 39 g total fat, 61 mg cholesterol, 148 mg sodium*

### *Dinner on the Patio*

*When good friends gather on a warm summer evening, what could be more appealing than Cool Salmon Steaks & Vegetables with Radish Tartar Sauce (facing page). To accompany this one-dish entrée, bring along freshly baked Parmesan Cheese Bread (page 29).*

# Chile, Shrimp & Corn Salad

*Pictured on page 43*

◼◼◼

*Preparation time: 45 minutes*

*Chilling time: At least 1 hour*

If your potluck assignment is a salad, surprise them with this bold creation. First, you sauté shrimp with fresh corn and red bell pepper in chile-spiked oil. Then you toss it all with spinach and leaf lettuce for a result that's as pleasing to the eye as it is to the palate.

  3   **small dried hot red chiles**
  ¼   **cup olive oil or salad oil**
  ½   **teaspoon pepper**
  2   **cups corn cut from cob or 1 package (10 oz.) frozen whole-kernel corn, thawed and drained**
  1   **medium-size red bell pepper, seeded and finely chopped**
  1   **pound medium-size raw shrimp, shelled and deveined**
  1   **tablespoon soy sauce**
  ⅔   **cup cider vinegar**
  1   **pound spinach**
  1   **pound green leaf lettuce, washed and crisped**

In a wide frying pan, combine chiles and oil; cook, stirring, over medium heat until chiles are lightly browned (about 4 minutes). Add pepper, corn, and bell pepper; increase heat to high and cook, stirring constantly, until vegetables are tender to bite (about 3 minutes). Add shrimp and cook, stirring, just until shrimp turn light pink (about 3 more minutes).

Remove pan from heat. Stir in soy sauce and vinegar; spoon shrimp mixture into a bowl. Let cool; then cover and refrigerate for at least 1 hour or for up to 4 hours.

Meanwhile, wash spinach, remove and discard stems, and pat dry. Tear spinach and lettuce into bite-size pieces (you should have about 4 quarts total, lightly packed). Transport shrimp mixture and greens separately in a cooler.

To serve, lift chiles from shrimp mixture to use for garnish, or discard. Place greens in a large salad bowl; spoon shrimp mixture over. Mix lightly. Makes 6 to 8 servings.

*Per serving: 174 calories, 13 g protein, 14 g carbohydrates, 9 g total fat, 70 mg cholesterol, 241 mg sodium*

# Cool Salmon Steaks & Vegetables

*Pictured on facing page*

◼◼◼

*Preparation time: 25 minutes*

*Cooking time: 45 minutes*

Poached salmon, cool and succulent, occupies center stage on this potluck platter.

  1½   **pounds green beans**
  6    **small salmon steaks (6 to 8 oz. *each*)**
  12   **to 18 small red thin-skinned potatoes**
       **Radish Tartar Sauce (recipe follows)**
  6    **to 8 butter lettuce leaves, washed and crisped**
  2    **cups cherry tomatoes**
       **Lemon wedges**

In a 6- to 8-quart pan, bring 4 quarts water to a boil over high heat. Add beans and cook just until bright green (about 5 minutes). Lift out beans and immerse in cold water until cool. Meanwhile, return water to a boil. Add salmon steaks, cover, and remove from heat. Let stand until fish is opaque throughout when cut (10 to 14 minutes). Lift out and immerse in cold water until cool.

Meanwhile, peel a narrow strip from each potato. Return water to a boil. Add potatoes; reduce heat, cover, and cook until tender when pierced (20 to 25 minutes). Drain; immerse in cold water until cool.

Meanwhile, prepare Radish Tartar Sauce.

Drain beans, fish, and potatoes. (At this point, you may cover and refrigerate separately for up to a day.) Transport vegetables, fish, and sauce separately in a cooler. To serve, line a platter with lettuce. Add fish, beans, potatoes, tomatoes, and lemon. Offer sauce to add to taste. Makes 6 servings.

***Radish Tartar Sauce.*** Mix ¾ cup *each* **plain yogurt** and **sour cream,** 1 cup chopped **radishes,** ½ cup thinly sliced **green onions** (including tops), 3 tablespoons drained **capers,** and 1½ tablespoons **prepared horseradish.** Season to taste with **salt.** If made ahead, cover and refrigerate for up to a day. Stir before serving. Makes about 2½ cups.

*Per serving: 465 calories, 50 g protein, 33 g carbohydrates, 15 g total fat, 125 mg cholesterol, 118 mg sodium*

*Per tablespoon sauce: 13 calories, .38 g protein, .68 g carbohydrate, .97 g total fat, 2 mg cholesterol, 23 mg sodium*

# Gravlax Plus

*Preparation time: 20 minutes*

*Chilling time: 24 hours*

In Sweden, salmon cured with dill and a mixture of salt and sugar is called *gravlax*. Curing draws moisture from the fish, firming its texture and introducing a distinctive flavor.

- 1 unskinned salmon, lingcod, or halibut fillet (about 2 lbs.)
- ¼ cup salad oil
- ⅓ cup *each* sugar and salt
- 1½ tablespoons whole white peppercorns, coarsely crushed
- ¼ cup cognac or brandy (optional)
- 1 small red onion, thinly sliced
- 2 to 3 cups lightly packed fresh dill sprigs
  Mustard Sauce (recipe follows)
  Lemon wedges
  Sour cream
  Rye, pumpernickel, or sourdough bread

Rub fish with oil. Mix sugar, salt, and peppercorns; lightly rub some of the mixture all over fish. Lay fish, skin side down, in a glass baking dish that fish almost fills. Pat remaining sugar mixture over fish; spoon cognac over, if desired.

Cover fish with onion slices and 1 to 2 cups of the dill. Cover tightly. Refrigerate for 12 hours, basting fish 3 or 4 times with accumulated juices. Turn fish over, placing dill and onion underneath. Cover and refrigerate for 12 more hours, basting 3 or 4 more times. After 24 hours, fish is ready to serve. If made ahead, refrigerate in brine for up to a day. To store for 2 more days, remove from brine and pat dry; enclose fish, dill, and onion in a plastic bag and refrigerate.

Just before leaving for potluck, prepare Mustard Sauce.

Discard dill and onion. Transport fish in a cooler. To serve, place fish, skin side down, on a serving board. Garnish with lemon wedges and remaining dill. Cut fish into paper-thin slanting slices. Offer sauce, sour cream, and bread as accompaniments. Makes 10 to 12 servings.

*Mustard Sauce.* Combine ⅔ cup **Dijon mustard,** ½ cup **salad oil,** 1½ tablespoons **white wine vinegar,** and 1 tablespoon **sugar.** Mix until well blended. Stir in ¼ cup chopped **fresh dill** and season to taste with **pepper.** Makes about 1¼ cups.

*Per serving gravlax: 145 calories, 15 g protein, 4 g carbohydrates, 7 g total fat, 42 mg cholesterol, 1530 mg sodium*

*Per tablespoon sauce: 61 calories, .06 g protein, 2 g carbohydrates, 6 g total fat, 0 mg cholesterol, 239 mg sodium*

# Cool Poached Fish with Sauce

*Preparation time: 35 minutes*

*Chilling time: At least 2 hours*

A smooth sauce of green peppercorns and avocado accompanies these poached fish fillets. The sauce is also good as a dip for crisp raw vegetables.

- About 2 cups *each* water and dry white wine
- 1½ teaspoons salt
- 8 whole black peppercorns
- 1 small onion, cut into chunks
- 4 to 6 parsley sprigs
- 2½ to 3 pounds firm white-fleshed fish fillets, such as lingcod or rockfish
  Creamy Avocado Sauce (recipe follows)
  Lettuce leaves, washed and crisped
  Lemon wedges

In a wide frying pan, combine 2 cups each of the water and wine, salt, peppercorns, onion, and parsley. Cover and simmer for about 20 minutes. Place fish fillets in a single layer in pan without crowding. If necessary, add equal parts more water and wine until liquid just covers fish. Cover and simmer until fish is opaque throughout when cut (about 10 minutes for each inch of thickness). Remove fish with a slotted spatula and let cool. Cover and refrigerate for at least 2 hours or for up to a day.

Meanwhile, prepare Creamy Avocado Sauce.

Transport fish, sauce, lettuce, and lemon wedges separately in a cooler. To serve, line a platter with lettuce. Arrange fish over lettuce and garnish with lemon wedges. Offer sauce to add to taste. Makes 6 servings.

*Creamy Avocado Sauce.* In a blender or food processor, combine 1 **egg;** 1½ tablespoons **bottled green peppercorns,** rinsed and drained; ¾ teaspoon **salt;** ¼ cup **lemon juice;** 3 tablespoons half-and-half; and 2 softly ripe **avocados,** pitted, peeled, and cut into chunks. Whirl until smooth. If made ahead, cover and refrigerate for up to 3 hours. Makes about 2½ cups.

*Per serving fish: 196 calories, 40 g protein, .68 g carbohydrate, 2 g total fat, 118 mg cholesterol, 256 mg sodium*

*Per tablespoon sauce: 21 calories, .39 g protein, 1 g carbohydrate, 2 g total fat, 7 mg cholesterol, 45 mg sodium*

## Red Snapper Casserole

*Preparation time: 30 minutes*

*Baking time: 35 to 45 minutes*

Hot and creamy, this fish and potato casserole contains a layer of tart sauerkraut.

- 4 medium-size thin-skinned potatoes (about 2 lbs. *total*)
- ¼ cup butter or margarine
- 2 large onions, finely chopped
- ¼ cup all-purpose flour
- 1 cup *each* milk and regular-strength chicken broth
  Salt and pepper
- 2 pounds firm white-fleshed fish fillets, such as red snapper or rock cod
- 1 can (16 oz.) sauerkraut, well drained
  Paprika

Place potatoes on a rack over about 1 inch boiling water. Cover and steam until tender when pierced (about 25 minutes); let cool.

In a 3- to 4-quart pan, melt butter over medium heat. Add onions and cook, stirring, until soft (8 to 10 minutes). Sprinkle with flour; cook, stirring, until bubbly. Remove from heat and gradually stir in milk and broth. Cook, stirring, until sauce boils and thickens. Season to taste with salt and pepper.

Peel potatoes, if desired; slice and arrange in a shallow 3-quart baking dish. Top with a third of the sauce. Add fish and another third of the sauce. Top with sauerkraut and remaining sauce; sprinkle lightly with paprika. (At this point, you may cover and refrigerate for up to 4 hours.) Transport in a cooler. Bake, covered, in a 350° oven until fish is opaque throughout when cut (35 to 45 minutes). Makes 8 to 10 servings.

*Per serving: 252 calories, 23 g protein, 24 g carbohydrates, 7 g total fat, 49 mg cholesterol, 523 mg sodium*

## Seafood Chowder for a Crowd

*Preparation time: 25 minutes*

*Cooking time: About 45 minutes*

Three kinds of seafood—shrimp, clams, and halibut—make this rich red chowder a one-pot banquet. To complement the green chile salsa that boldly seasons the soup, you may want to offer a pan of cornbread or a basket of warm corn sticks.

- ¼ pound bacon, cut into ½-inch pieces
- 3 medium-size carrots, sliced ¼ inch thick
- 1 cup thinly sliced celery
- 2 small thin-skinned potatoes (*each* about 2 inches in diameter), cut into ¾-inch cubes
- 1 medium-size onion, finely chopped
- 1 medium-size red or green bell pepper, seeded and finely chopped
- 2 cans (15 oz. *each*) tomato sauce
- 2 cups water
- 1 bottle (8 oz.) clam juice
- 1 jar (12 oz.) mild green chile salsa
- ¾ pound boned, skinned halibut, cut into ½-inch cubes
- ¾ pound small cooked shrimp
- 2 cans (6½ oz. *each*) chopped clams
  Salt and pepper

In a 6- to 8-quart pan, cook bacon over medium heat until crisp. Discard all but about 3 tablespoons of the drippings; stir in carrots, celery, potatoes, onion, and bell pepper. Cook, stirring often, for 10 minutes.

Stir in tomato sauce, water, clam juice, and salsa. Bring to a boil; reduce heat, cover, and simmer until vegetables are tender when pierced (about 25 minutes). Let cool. (At this point, you may cover and refrigerate for up to 8 hours.) Transport chowder, halibut, and shrimp separately in a cooler.

Just before serving, bring chowder to a gentle boil over medium heat. Stir in clams and their liquid and halibut; cover and simmer until fish is opaque throughout when cut (about 2 minutes). Remove chowder from heat; add shrimp and season to taste with salt and pepper. Makes 8 servings.

*Per serving: 249 calories, 25 g protein, 20 g carbohydrates, 8 g total fat, 118 mg cholesterol, 1470 mg sodium*

## Crêpe Shrimp Stack

*Pictured on facing page*

■

*Preparation time: 40 minutes*

*Baking time: 30 to 35 minutes*

For a festive brunch, consider this showy crêpe-based entrée you can prepare ahead.

- 8 **Crêpes (recipe follows)**
- 7 **ounces (about 1 cup) creamy garlic-herb cheese, at room temperature**
- ½ **pound small cooked shrimp**
- 3 **tablespoons thinly sliced chives or green onions (including tops)**
- 2½ **cups (10 oz.) shredded jack cheese**
   **Watercress sprigs**

Prepare Crêpes. Spread a crêpe with about 2 tablespoons of the garlic-herb cheese. Place crêpe, cheese side up, on a rimmed ovenproof platter or in a shallow 9- to 11-inch round casserole.

Lightly mix shrimp, chives, and 2¼ cups of the jack cheese. Sprinkle about ½ cup of the shrimp mixture over cheese-spread crêpe. Repeat with remaining crêpes, garlic-herb cheese, and shrimp mixture, ending with a crêpe. Sprinkle with remaining ¼ cup jack cheese. (At this point, you may cover and refrigerate for up to a day.) Transport crêpes and watercress separately in a cooler.

Bake crêpes, uncovered, in a 350° oven until hot (30 to 35 minutes). Garnish with watercress. Cut into wedges to serve. Makes 6 servings.

*Crêpes.* In a blender or food processor, combine 2 **eggs** and ½ cup **all-purpose flour;** whirl until smooth. Blend in ⅔ cup **milk.**

Heat a 6- to 7-inch crêpe or other flat-bottomed frying pan over medium heat until a drop of water dances in pan. Add ¼ teaspoon **butter** or margarine, tilting pan to coat bottom. Pour a scant ¼ cup of the batter all at once into center of pan, swiftly tilting pan so batter flows over entire surface.

Cook until lightly browned on bottom (30 to 40 seconds). Turn and cook until other side is browned (about 20 seconds). Let cool. Repeat to make additional crêpes, adding more butter as needed and stirring batter occasionally. If made ahead, cover and refrigerate for up to 2 days. Bring to room temperature before separating. Makes 8 crêpes.

*Per serving: 422 calories, 26 g protein, 11 g carbohydrates, 30 g total fat, 250 mg cholesterol, 486 mg sodium*

## Tuna & Spaghetti Bake

■

*Preparation time: 40 minutes*

*Baking time: 40 to 45 minutes*

Over a crust of cooked spaghetti, this delightful savory pie features a dill-accented filling of tuna, spinach, and cottage cheese, with a gilding of Swiss cheese on top. Alongside, offer a sliced avocado and orange salad and a loaf of hot garlic bread.

- 8 **ounces spaghetti**
- 6 **tablespoons butter or margarine**
- ⅔ **cup grated Parmesan cheese**
- 1 **large onion, finely chopped**
- 2 **packages (10 oz. *each*) frozen chopped spinach, thawed**
- 1 **teaspoon *each* dill weed and garlic salt**
- 1½ **tablespoons Dijon mustard**
- 3 **cans (6½ oz. *each*) chunk-style tuna, drained and flaked**
- 2 **cups small curd cottage cheese**
- 2 **cups (8 oz.) shredded Swiss cheese**
- 4 **eggs, well beaten**

In a 4- to 5-quart pan, cook spaghetti in 3 quarts boiling water until tender to bite (8 to 10 minutes). Or cook according to package directions. Drain well.

Melt 4 tablespoons of the butter. In a large bowl, mix spaghetti, melted butter, and Parmesan cheese. Spread in a greased 9- by 13-inch baking dish; set aside.

In a wide frying pan, melt remaining 2 tablespoons butter over medium heat. Add onion and cook, stirring often, until soft but not browned (6 to 8 minutes). Meanwhile, squeeze out as much liquid as possible from spinach; set aside. Stir dill weed, garlic salt, and mustard into onion mixture. Remove from heat and mix in spinach, tuna, cottage cheese, and 1 cup of the Swiss cheese. Pour eggs evenly over spaghetti and spread with tuna mixture. (At this point, you may cover and refrigerate for up to 6 hours.) Transport in a cooler.

Bake, loosely covered, in a 350° oven until casserole is hot and eggs are set (35 to 40 minutes). Uncover, sprinkle with remaining 1 cup Swiss cheese, and continue baking until cheese is melted (about 5 more minutes). Cut into squares to serve. Makes 12 servings.

*Per serving: 378 calories, 30 g protein, 19 g carbohydrates, 20 g total fat, 141 mg cholesterol, 752 mg sodium*

**Come for Brunch**

*Temptingly topped with melted cheese, Crêpe Shrimp Stack (facing page) is cut into generous wedges for brunch. Easy menu contributions include a basketful of warmed croissants and a bowl of fresh summer fruits.*

# Poach Now, Bake Later Fish

Oven-poaching is a simple technique popular with European cooks for producing delicate fish entrées in convenient make-ahead steps. It works well with a variety of mild white-fleshed fish. You bake the fish in a little liquid and then use the liquid to make the sauce. The sauce masks and protects the fish while it's refrigerated and later while it heats.

## Oven-poached Fish

2 pounds lingcod, rockfish, sole, halibut, sea bass, or Greenland turbot fillets (*each* up to 1 inch thick)
½ cup regular-strength chicken broth or dry white wine
1 tablespoon lemon juice
Salt
Additional regular-strength chicken broth or dry white wine (if needed)

Arrange fish fillets, side by side, in a shallow casserole or baking pan just large enough to hold them in a single layer. If fillets are less than ½ inch thick, fold in half crosswise.

Pour broth and lemon juice over fish; sprinkle lightly with salt. Cover and bake in a 400° oven until fish is opaque throughout when cut (10 minutes for thin pieces, up to 22 minutes for thick pieces). Let cool slightly.

Holding fish in place with a wide spatula or pan lid, drain fish liquid into a measuring cup (you should have about 1 cup, but this varies with type of fish). Cover and refrigerate fish until cool.

If necessary, boil fish liquid to reduce to 1 cup, or add broth or wine to make 1 cup. Reserve for sauce.

## Baked Fish with Horseradish Cream Sauce

Oven-poached Fish (cooked in chicken broth; see at left)
3 tablespoons butter or margarine
2 tablespoons all-purpose flour
⅓ cup half-and-half
1 tablespoon prepared horseradish
Finely chopped parsley

Prepare Oven-poached Fish.

In a 1- to 1½-quart pan, melt butter over medium heat. Blend in flour and cook, stirring, until bubbly. Remove from heat and gradually add the 1 cup reserved fish liquid, half-and-half, and horseradish. Return to heat and cook, stirring constantly, until mixture boils and thickens (1 to 2 minutes). Let cool.

Spoon sauce over fish, covering completely. (At this point, you may cover and refrigerate for up to 8 hours.) Transport in a cooler.

Bake, uncovered, in a 400° oven until sauce bubbles around edges and fish is hot (10 to 12 minutes). Garnish with parsley. Makes 6 servings.

*Per serving: 210 calories, 28 g protein, 3 g carbohydrates, 9 g total fat, 99 mg cholesterol, 240 mg sodium*

## Baked Fish with Mushroom Sauce

*Pictured on page 94*

Oven-poached Fish (cooked in wine; see at left)
4 tablespoons butter or margarine
½ pound mushrooms, thinly sliced
2½ tablespoons all-purpose flour
½ cup half-and-half
⅛ teaspoon ground nutmeg
Salt
¾ cup shredded Swiss cheese

Prepare Oven-poached Fish.

In a 1½- to 2-quart pan, melt 2 tablespoons of the butter over medium-high heat. Add mushrooms and cook, stirring often, until juices have evaporated; lift out mushrooms and set aside.

In same pan, melt remaining 2 tablespoons butter over medium heat; blend in flour and cook, stirring, until bubbly. Remove from heat and gradually blend in the 1 cup reserved fish liquid, half-and-half, and nutmeg. Return to heat; cook, stirring constantly, until mixture boils and thickens (1 to 2 minutes). Remove from heat, add mushrooms, and season to taste with salt. Let cool.

Spoon sauce evenly over fish. Sprinkle with cheese. (At this point, you may cover and refrigerate for up to 8 hours.) Transport in a cooler. Bake, uncovered, in a 400° oven until cheese is melted (10 to 12 minutes). Makes 6 servings.

*Per serving: 301 calories, 33 g protein, 6 g carbohydrates, 16 g total fat, 120 mg cholesterol, 293 mg sodium*

# Scallop Lasagne

*Preparation time: 45 minutes*

*Baking time: 40 to 45 minutes*

This delicate seafood version of the popular pasta dish features scallops in a cream sauce.

- ⅓ cup butter or margarine
- 1 cup thinly sliced green onions (including tops)
- 1 clove garlic, minced or pressed
- ½ teaspoon fresh thyme leaves or ¼ teaspoon dry thyme
- 2 pounds bay scallops or thinly sliced sea scallops, rinsed and patted dry
- ⅓ cup all-purpose flour
- 1 cup *each* whipping cream and regular-strength chicken broth
- ½ cup dry vermouth or dry white wine
- 1 package (8 oz.) lasagne noodles
- 2 cups (8 oz.) shredded Swiss cheese

In a wide frying pan, melt 1 tablespoon of the butter over medium-high heat. Add green onions, garlic, and thyme; cook, stirring, for 1 minute. Add scallops and cook, stirring often, until opaque throughout when cut (2 to 3 minutes). Remove from heat and pour scallop mixture into a large strainer over a bowl; let drain for 20 minutes.

Meanwhile, in same pan, melt remaining butter over medium heat. Add flour and stir until light golden. Remove from heat and mix in cream, broth, and vermouth. Increase heat to high and bring to a boil, stirring constantly; set aside.

In a 6-quart pan, cook lasagne in 4 quarts boiling water just until tender to bite (about 10 minutes). Or cook according to package directions. Drain, rinse until cool, and drain again; set aside.

Pour juices drained from scallops into a 1- to 1½-quart pan and boil until reduced to about 2 tablespoons (stir near end). Add to sauce.

Line a greased 9- by 12-inch baking dish with a third of the lasagne. Layer with a third each of the sauce, scallop mixture, and cheese. Repeat two more times. Cover with foil. (At this point, you may refrigerate for up to a day.) Transport in a cooler.

Bake, covered, in a 350° oven for 20 minutes. Uncover and continue baking until golden (20 to 25 more minutes). Makes 6 to 8 servings.

*Per serving: 499 calories, 32 g protein, 33 g carbohydrates, 26 g total fat, 117 mg cholesterol, 472 mg sodium*

# Clam & Noodle Casserole

*Preparation time: 45 minutes*

*Baking time: 30 to 45 minutes*

Rosy tomato-flavored pasta, bright green spinach, and creamy white ricotta come together in this tri-color seafood casserole.

- 8 ounces dry tomato or spinach noodles
- 2 cans (6½ oz. *each*) minced clams
- ¼ cup butter or margarine
- ¼ cup all-purpose flour
- 1 bottle (8 oz.) clam juice
- 2 cloves garlic, minced or pressed
- 1 teaspoon Italian herb seasoning or ¼ teaspoon *each* dry basil, oregano, thyme, and marjoram
- ¼ cup finely chopped parsley
- 3 tablespoons lemon juice
- 1 pound ricotta cheese or 2 cups small curd cottage cheese
- 1 package (10 oz.) frozen chopped spinach, thawed
- 8 ounces jack cheese, thinly sliced
- ¼ cup grated Parmesan cheese

In a 6-quart pan, cook noodles in 4 quarts boiling water just until tender to bite (8 to 10 minutes). Or cook according to package directions. Drain, rinse with hot water, and drain again; set aside. Meanwhile, drain clams, reserving liquid.

In a 2- to 3-quart pan, melt butter over medium heat. Stir in flour and cook until bubbly. Remove from heat and gradually stir in clam juice and reserved liquid from minced clams. Cook, stirring, until mixture boils and thickens (about 5 minutes). Remove from heat and stir in clams, garlic, Italian herb seasoning, parsley, and lemon juice.

Line a greased 9- by 12-inch baking dish with a third of the noodles. Evenly layer with ricotta, a third of the clam sauce, and half the remaining noodles. Squeeze out as much liquid as possible from spinach; layer over noodles. Top with half the jack cheese and half the remaining clam sauce. Finally, add remaining noodles, jack cheese, and clam sauce; sprinkle with Parmesan cheese. (At this point, you may cover and refrigerate for up to a day.) Transport in a cooler.

Bake, uncovered, in a 350° oven until bubbly and hot (30 to 45 minutes). Makes 6 to 8 servings.

*Per serving: 407 calories, 24 g protein, 30 g carbohydrates, 22 g total fat, 101 mg cholesterol, 687 mg sodium*

**By the Sea**

*Satisfy hearty appetites at the beach with (clockwise from top right) Oregonian
Turkey Chili (page 69), Turkey & Mint-Avocado Pinwheels (page 68), and
Sourdough Chili Chicken Salad (page 57).*

# Poultry

Both delicious flavor and reasonable price account in part for poultry's popularity as a main dish. But it's the versatility of chicken and turkey that means even more to the cook seeking a new and unusual potluck rendition. For a summer luncheon, will it be a fruited chicken salad or avocado-accented turkey pinwheel sandwiches? Or to banish winter's chill, how about a piquant Mexican-influenced chicken entrée or an Italian-inspired turkey casserole? No matter what the season or occasion, poultry remains a perennial potluck favorite.

## Curry & Fruit Chicken Salad

*Preparation time: 30 minutes*

*Chilling time: At least 1 hour*

Fresh pineapple, a rosy apple, and raisins sweeten chicken in this main-dish salad accented with roasted peanuts and candied ginger. Choose sour cream or plain yogurt for the base of the dilled curry dressing.

    **Dill-Curry Dressing (recipe follows)**
1  **medium-size red apple**
3  **cups cooked chicken, cut into ½-inch-wide strips**
2  **cups thinly sliced celery**
¾  **cup dry-roasted salted peanuts**
½  **cup raisins**
1  **small pineapple (about 3 lbs.)**
8  **to 10 large lettuce leaves, washed and crisped**
2  **tablespoons minced candied ginger (optional)**

Prepare Dill-Curry Dressing.

Cut apple lengthwise into thin slivers and combine with chicken, celery, ½ cup of the peanuts, raisins, and dressing in a large bowl. Mix gently until blended. (At this point, you may cover and refrigerate for up to a day.)

Peel and slice pineapple. Arrange lettuce on a platter; top with pineapple and then chicken salad. Sprinkle with remaining ¼ cup peanuts and, if desired, candied ginger. Transport in a cooler. Makes 4 to 6 servings.

***Dill-Curry Dressing.*** Combine 1 cup **sour cream** or plain yogurt, 2 tablespoons **lemon juice,** 1½ teaspoons **curry powder,** and ½ teaspoon **dill weed.** Mix until well blended. Cover and refrigerate for at least 1 hour or for up to 2 days.

*Per serving: 437 calories, 27 g protein, 36 g carbohydrates, 23 g total fat, 79 mg cholesterol, 280 mg sodium*

# Mustard-Chicken Waldorf Salad

*Preparation time: 30 minutes*

For exceptional elegance, dress this colorful Waldorf salad with your own fresh mayonnaise made with Dijon and coarse-grain mustards. It's a snap when you use a blender or food processor.

    Fresh Mayonnaise (recipe follows)
1   large stalk celery, finely chopped
1   tablespoon drained capers
2   tablespoons chopped walnuts
¼   cup *each* coarse-grain mustard and Dijon
    mustard
3   cups cooked chicken, cut into ½-inch-wide
    strips
2   medium-size Red Delicious apples
    Salt and pepper
3   tablespoons lemon juice
1   large head butter lettuce (about ½ lb.), washed
    and crisped
1   small head radicchio (about 2½ oz.), washed and
    crisped
    Parsley sprigs

Prepare Fresh Mayonnaise.

In a large bowl, combine celery, capers, walnuts, coarse-grain mustard, Dijon mustard, and chicken. Peel and dice one of the apples; add to chicken mixture along with ½ cup of the mayonnaise. Mix lightly until blended. Season to taste with salt and pepper. (At this point, you may cover and refrigerate for up to a day.)

Thinly slice remaining apple and mix with lemon juice. Arrange butter lettuce and radicchio on a platter. Mound salad on greens. Garnish with apple slices and parsley. Transport salad and remaining mayonnaise separately in a cooler. Offer mayonnaise to add to taste. Makes 4 to 6 servings.

*Fresh Mayonnaise.* In a blender or food processor, combine 1 **egg,** 2 tablespoons **sherry vinegar** or red wine vinegar, and 1 tablespoon *each* **Dijon mustard** and **coarse-grain mustard.** Whirl until well blended (3 to 5 seconds). With motor running, add 1 cup **salad oil,** a few drops at a time at first, then increasing to a slow, steady stream about ¹⁄₁₆ inch wide. (Add oil as slowly as possible.) Cover and refrigerate. If made ahead, mayonnaise may be refrigerated for up to 2 weeks. Makes about 1⅓ cups.

*Per serving salad: 338 calories, 22 g protein, 12 g carbohydrates, 23 g total fat, 80 mg cholesterol, 548 mg sodium*

*Per tablespoon mayonnaise: 97 calories, .32 g protein, .20 g carbohydrate, 11 g total fat, 13 mg cholesterol, 32 mg sodium*

# Chicken-Spinach Salad with Cilantro

*Preparation time: 25 minutes*

*Marinating time: At least 4 hours*

If you're going to a potluck tomorrow, roast two chickens tonight—one for dinner and the other to make a salad with fresh spinach and marinated garbanzo beans and red onion rings.

    Cilantro Dressing (recipe follows)
1   can (15 oz.) garbanzo beans, drained
1   small red onion, thinly sliced and separated
    into rings
1   can (2¼ oz.) sliced ripe olives, drained
1   bunch spinach (about ¾ lb.)
3   cups cooked chicken, cut into ½-inch-wide
    strips

Prepare Cilantro Dressing and add garbanzo beans, onion, and olives. Mix gently until blended. Cover and refrigerate for at least 4 hours or until next day. Meanwhile, wash spinach leaves, pat dry, and refrigerate for at least 30 minutes.

Lightly mix chicken into garbanzo mixture. Arrange spinach on a rimmed platter and top with chicken salad. Transport in a cooler. Makes 4 to 6 servings.

*Cilantro Dressing.* In a large bowl, combine ¾ cup **salad oil,** 6 tablespoons **white wine vinegar,** 1½ teaspoons **dry marjoram,** ½ teaspoon **salt,** and ⅓ to ½ cup finely chopped **fresh cilantro** (coriander). Mix until well blended.

*Per serving: 495 calories, 26 g protein, 19 g carbohydrates, 36 g total fat, 62 mg cholesterol, 580 mg sodium*

# Sourdough Chili Chicken Salad

*Pictured on page 54*

*Preparation time: 35 minutes*

*Chilling time: At least 1 hour*

An edible sourdough bread bowl conveniently transports this bold chicken salad to an informal potluck. En route, the bread soaks up flavor from the dressing. Save the bread you hollow out to make croutons or a buttery crumb topping for your next potluck casserole.

> 2 **oblong sourdough loaves (1 lb.** *each***) or 1 round sourdough loaf (24 oz.)**
> **Chili Dressing (recipe follows)**
> 1 **can (12 oz.) whole-kernel corn with sweet peppers, drained**
> ¾ **cup sliced radishes**
> 1 **can (4 oz.) diced green chiles, drained**
> 1 **cup (4 oz.) matchstick pieces jack cheese**
> 2 **carrots, shredded**
> ¼ **cup thinly sliced green onions (including tops)**
> 1½ **cups diced cooked chicken**

Cut a ½- to ¾-inch-thick slice from top crust of each loaf to form a lid; set aside. Pull out bread from center of loaves to form a bowl about ⅜ inch thick. (Wrap bread torn from center and freeze for another use.)

Prepare Chili Dressing.

In a large bowl, combine corn, radishes, chiles, cheese, carrots, green onions, and chicken. Add all but 2 tablespoons of the dressing and mix lightly until blended. Spoon salad mixture into bread bowls. Drizzle reserved dressing over cut sides of lids; then place on loaves. Wrap well and refrigerate for at least 1 hour or for up to 4 hours. Transport in a cooler.

To serve, cut long loaves into large pieces (cut round loaf into wedges). Makes 6 servings.

*Chili Dressing.* Combine ½ cup **salad oil,** ¼ cup **wine vinegar,** 1 teaspoon **chili powder,** ½ teaspoon **garlic salt,** ¼ teaspoon **ground cumin,** a dash of **ground red pepper** (cayenne), and ½ cup chopped **fresh cilantro** (coriander). Mix until well blended.

*Per serving: 527 calories, 22 g protein, 47 g carbohydrates, 29 g total fat, 49 mg cholesterol, 944 mg sodium*

# Overnight Layered Chicken Salad

*Pictured on page 59*

*Preparation time: 35 minutes*

*Chilling time: At least 8 hours*

This ample salad serves as many as a dozen at a potluck lunch or supper. Bring along some buttery croissants or crusty rolls to offer alongside.

> 6 **cups shredded iceberg lettuce**
> ¼ **pound bean sprouts**
> 1 **can (8 oz.) water chestnuts, drained and sliced**
> ½ **cup thinly sliced green onions (including tops)**
> 1 **medium-size cucumber, thinly sliced**
> 4 **cups cooked chicken, cut into ½-inch-wide strips**
> 2 **packages (6 oz.** *each***) frozen Chinese pea pods (also called snow or sugar peas), thawed**
> 2 **cups mayonnaise**
> 2 **teaspoons curry powder**
> 1 **tablespoon sugar**
> ½ **teaspoon ground ginger**
> ½ **cup Spanish-style peanuts**
> 12 **to 18 cherry tomatoes, halved**

Spread lettuce in an even layer in a 4-quart bowl. Top with layers of bean sprouts, water chestnuts, green onions, cucumber, and chicken. Pat pea pods dry and arrange on top.

In a bowl, stir together mayonnaise, curry powder, sugar, and ginger. Spread evenly over salad. Cover and refrigerate for at least 8 hours or for up to a day.

Sprinkle salad with peanuts and arrange tomatoes around edge of bowl. Transport in a cooler. To serve, use a spoon and fork to lift out some of each layer. Makes 10 to 12 servings.

*Per serving: 428 calories, 18 g protein, 11 g carbohydrates, 36 g total fat, 63 mg cholesterol, 283 mg sodium*

## Cuban Chicken Stew

Preparation time: 1 hour

Baking time: 1½ to 2 hours

Raisins and olives lend a Cuban accent to this substantial stew. It takes time to prepare, but once in the oven, the spicy one-dish meal needs no further attention. Simple accompaniments are a green salad and crusty bread.

4½ to 5 pounds meaty chicken pieces, such as breasts, thighs, and legs
2 tablespoons olive oil or salad oil
2 medium-size onions, thinly sliced
1 *each* red and green bell pepper, seeded and finely chopped
4 cloves garlic, minced or pressed
1½ teaspoons *each* dry oregano and ground cumin
2 cans (15 oz. *each*) tomato sauce
½ cup dry white wine or regular-strength chicken broth
8 small red thin-skinned potatoes (about 1½ lbs. *total*)
1 cup *each* raisins and pitted ripe olives
2 cups frozen peas, thawed
Salt

Rinse chicken pieces and pat dry. Cut breast halves, if used, in half crosswise. Heat oil in a wide frying pan over medium heat. Add chicken, 4 or 5 pieces at a time (do not crowd), and cook until well browned on all sides. Remove pieces as they brown and transfer to a deep 5- to 6-quart casserole. When all chicken is browned, pour off and discard all but 2 tablespoons of the drippings.

Add onions and bell peppers to drippings in pan. Cook, stirring often, until onions are soft but not browned. Stir in garlic, oregano, and cumin; then add tomato sauce and wine. Cook, stirring often, until sauce comes to a boil. Boil gently, uncovered, for 5 minutes.

Peel potatoes, if desired, and cut into quarters. Add to chicken with raisins and olives. Pour sauce over chicken. (At this point, you may cover and refrigerate for up to a day.)

Bake, covered, in a 375° oven until meat near bone is no longer pink when slashed and potatoes are tender (1½ to 2 hours). Stir in peas. Insulate to transport hot (see page 5). Offer salt to add to taste. Makes 12 to 15 servings.

*Per serving: 297 calories, 22 g protein, 25 g carbohydrates, 13 g total fat, 59 mg cholesterol, 492 mg sodium*

## Chicken Florentine

Preparation time: 35 minutes

Cooking time: 45 minutes

Baking time: 10 to 15 minutes

Fresh, easy, and delicious, this baked ensemble of chicken and spinach feeds up to a dozen with no last-minute fuss.

3 cups regular-strength chicken broth
1½ cups dry white wine
3 or 4 parsley sprigs
1 bay leaf
1 teaspoon dry thyme
6 whole chicken breasts (about 1 lb. *each*), skinned, boned, and split
¼ cup butter or margarine
1 tablespoon Dijon mustard
3 tablespoons all-purpose flour
¾ cup lightly packed shredded Gruyère or Swiss cheese
3½ to 4 pounds spinach
3 tablespoons grated Parmesan cheese

In a 5- to 6-quart pan, combine broth, wine, parsley, bay leaf, and thyme. Add chicken and bring to a boil over high heat; cover pan and remove from heat. Let stand until chicken is no longer pink in thickest part when slashed (about 20 minutes). Lift chicken from broth mixture; set aside. Pour broth through a fine strainer into a bowl; discard herbs. Rinse pan. Return broth to pan and boil, uncovered, until reduced to 2½ cups (10 to 15 minutes).

In a 2- to 3-quart pan, melt butter over medium heat. Whisk in mustard and flour until smooth; then gradually whisk in broth. Cook until sauce boils and thickens. Remove from heat. Add Gruyère, stirring until smooth; set aside.

Grease 2 baking pans or oval casseroles. Discard spinach stems. Rinse leaves well and pat dry. Firmly press half the spinach into each pan. Arrange half the chicken in each. (At this point, you may cover cheese sauce and chicken and refrigerate separately for up to a day.)

Spoon sauce over chicken and spinach. Sprinkle with Parmesan cheese. Transport in a cooler.

Bake, uncovered, in a 450° oven until cheese is lightly browned (10 to 15 minutes). Makes 12 servings.

*Per serving: 279 calories, 41 g protein, 6 g carbohydrates, 10 g total fat, 106 mg cholesterol, 562 mg sodium*

### Bridge Club Buffet

*As triumphant as a grand slam, this elegant luncheon menu offers Overnight
Layered Chicken Salad (page 57), rolls and butter, and, for dessert,
Sour Cream Pound Cake (page 88).*

# Holiday Turkey Dinner

*Sharing efforts and expense can make a big holiday meal easier and more fun. Often, the best approach is to have the host cook the turkey while the guests bring the rest of the dishes ready to serve—hot or cold. One such menu is suggested here. Recipes for all except the roast turkey and stuffing follow.*

Shrimp on Palm Pedestals

Roast Turkey
with Stuffing & Gravy

Sweet Potatoes with Fresh
Candied Orange

Potatoes Romanoff

Broccoli Milanese

Cranberry-Port Relish

Pumpkin Cheesecake

*Each dish serves eight; when paired with a 12- to 15-pound turkey, there will be enough food to satisfy everyone.*

## Shrimp on Palm Pedestals

1   can (14 oz.) hearts of palm, drained and rinsed
¼   cup mayonnaise
1   teaspoon minced fresh dill or ¼ teaspoon dill weed
1   teaspoon lemon juice
¼   pound small cooked shrimp
    Dill sprigs (optional)

Cut hearts of palm into ¾-inch lengths and place, cut sides up, on a small tray.

In a small bowl, mix mayonnaise, minced dill, and lemon juice. Equally spoon mayonnaise mixture on each palm piece; top each with a shrimp and, if desired, a tiny dill sprig. If made ahead, cover and refrigerate for up to a day. Transport in a cooler. Makes 8 first-course servings.

*Per serving: 74 calories, 4 g protein, 2 g carbohydrates, 6 g total fat, 32 mg cholesterol, 71 mg sodium*

## Sweet Potatoes with Fresh Candied Orange

About 6 medium-size sweet potatoes or yams (3½ to 4 lbs. total)
4   large oranges
½   cup sugar
¼   cup orange-flavored liqueur
1   cup orange juice (if needed)
    Orange slices (optional)
    Fresh mint leaves (optional)

Arrange potatoes in a shallow rimmed baking pan. Bake, uncovered, in a 350° oven until soft (about 1 hour). When cool enough to handle, peel and place in a large bowl; set aside.

With a vegetable peeler, pare orange part only from the 4 oranges. Cut peel into strips about ¹⁄₁₆ inch wide. Ream oranges and set juice aside.

Place strips of orange peel in a 4- to 5-quart pan with 3 cups water. Bring to a boil over high heat; drain water. Add 3 more cups water, bring to a boil again, and drain water. Repeat a third

time. To candy orange peel, add sugar and 1 more cup water to pan. Boil over high heat, uncovered, until water is almost gone; watch carefully to avoid scorching. Add liqueur and boil until liquid is almost gone. Add ¼ cup of the reserved orange juice and bring to a boil, stirring. Remove from heat; set aside about 2 tablespoons of the candied peel.

Add remaining orange juice reamed from the 4 oranges and boil over high heat, uncovered, until reduced to 1 cup. Pour mixture into potatoes and mash. If potatoes are dry, add orange juice as needed to give a moist texture. Spoon potatoes into a shallow 2½- to 3-quart baking dish. (At this point, you may cover and refrigerate for up to a day.)

Bake, uncovered, in a 350° over until hot (about 1 hour). Insulate to transport hot (see page 5). To serve, garnish with reserved candied orange peel and, if desired, orange slices and mint leaves. Makes 8 servings.

*Per serving: 256 calories, 3 g protein, 61 g carbohydrates, .59 g total fat, 0 mg cholesterol, 22 mg sodium*

## Potatoes Romanoff

3   large russet potatoes (about 2 lbs. total)
2   cups large curd cottage cheese
1   cup sour cream
1   clove garlic, minced or pressed
¼   cup thinly sliced green onions (including tops)
    Salt
1   cup (4 oz.) shredded sharp Cheddar cheese
    Paprika

Cut potatoes into quarters and place in a 3- to 4-quart pan; add enough water to cover. Bring to a boil over high heat. Cover and boil gently until tender when pierced (about 25 minutes); drain and let cool.

Peel potatoes and cut into ¼-inch cubes. In a large bowl, combine potatoes, cottage cheese, sour cream, garlic, and green onions. Mix well; season to taste with salt. Spoon into a shallow 2- to 2½-quart casserole. Sprinkle with Cheddar cheese and dust decoratively with paprika. (At this point, you may cover and refrigerate for up to a day.)

Bake, covered, in a 350° oven until hot (about 1 hour). Insulate to transport hot (see page 5). Makes 8 servings.

*Per serving: 264 calories, 13 g protein, 23 g carbohydrates, 13 g total fat, 35 mg cholesterol, 323 mg sodium*

## Broccoli Milanese

½ cup olive oil
3 cloves garlic, minced or pressed
½ cup fine dry bread crumbs
¼ cup finely chopped parsley
½ teaspoon grated lemon peel
2 pounds broccoli
2 tablespoons lemon juice
Salt and pepper

In a small frying pan, combine ¼ cup of the olive oil and garlic over medium-high heat. Cook, stirring often, until garlic is pale golden. Add bread crumbs and cook, stirring, until richly toasted. Stir in parsley and lemon peel. Let cool; then package airtight and let stand for up to a day.

Trim and discard broccoli stem ends. Cut stalks, through flowerets, into ½-inch-thick pieces. In a 5- to 6-quart pan, bring about 3 inches water to a boil over

high heat. Add broccoli and boil gently, uncovered, just until tender when pierced (6 to 8 minutes). Drain, immerse in cold water until cool, and drain again. (At this point, you may cover and refrigerate for up to a day.)

Mix remaining ¼ cup oil with lemon juice; cover and let stand until ready to serve. Transport broccoli in a serving dish. Just before serving, drizzle oil mixture over broccoli and sprinkle with crumb mixture. Offer salt and pepper to add to taste. Serve at room temperature. Makes 8 servings.

*Per serving: 166 calories, 3 g protein, 9 g carbohydrates, 14 g total fat, .31 mg cholesterol, 66 mg sodium*

## Cranberry-Port Relish

3 cups (12-oz. package) fresh or frozen cranberries
1 medium-size onion, finely chopped
⅓ cup cider vinegar
1 cup *each* golden raisins and sugar
1½ cups port
½ teaspoon ground nutmeg
1 teaspoon *each* ground ginger and ground cinnamon

In a 3- to 4-quart pan, combine cranberries, onion, vinegar, raisins, sugar, port, nutmeg, ginger, and cinnamon. Bring to a boil over high heat, stirring occasionally. Reduce heat and simmer, uncovered, until relish is thick and reduced to 3 cups (about 30 minutes); stir often as relish thickens to prevent scorching. Let cool. If made ahead, cover and refrigerate for up to 2 weeks. Makes 8 servings.

*Per serving: 200 calories, 1 g protein, 52 g carbohydrates, .24 g total fat, 0 mg cholesterol, 7 mg sodium*

## Pumpkin Cheesecake

Graham Cracker Crust (recipe follows)
2 large packages (8 oz. *each*) cream cheese, at room temperature
¾ cup firmly packed brown sugar
1 can (1 lb.) pumpkin
2 teaspoons pumpkin pie spice
2 eggs
Sweetened whipped cream
Pecan halves

Prepare Graham Cracker Crust; set aside.

Meanwhile, in the large bowl of an electric mixer, beat cream cheese and brown sugar until blended. Blend in pumpkin and pumpkin pie spice. Add eggs and beat well. Pour filling into prepared crust.

Bake in a 350° oven until cheesecake barely jiggles in center when gently shaken (about 50 minutes). Let cool on a rack. Cover lightly and refrigerate for at least 3 hours or for up to a day.

Remove pan sides and garnish with whipped cream and pecans. Transport in a cooler. Makes 8 servings.

*Graham Cracker Crust.* Mix 1¾ cups **graham cracker crumbs,** 2 tablespoons **sugar,** and 3 tablespoons **butter** or margarine, melted. Press mixture over bottom and about 1 inch up sides of a 9-inch spring-form or cake pan with a removable bottom. Bake in a 350° oven until lightly browned (about 10 minutes). Let cool on a rack.

*Per serving: 471 calories, 8 g protein, 49 g carbohydrates, 27 g total fat, 143 mg cholesterol, 396 mg sodium*

**Proud Contributions**

*Three distinctive recipes from three different kitchens await your pleasure (clockwise from top): Eggroll Cannelloni with Chicken-Prosciutto Filling (facing page), Artichoke Hearts with Blue Cheese (page 20), and Spinach Salad with Basil Dressing (page 24).*

## Eggroll Cannelloni

*Pictured on facing page*

◆◆

*Preparation time: 1½ hours*

*Baking time: 30 to 40 minutes*

Marco Polo first brought pasta from the Orient to Europe. Here, we reverse direction, introducing a classic Italian filling and sauce to China's egg roll skins.

**Chicken-Prosciutto Filling (recipe follows)**
**Creamy Tomato-Mint Sauce (recipe follows)**
12 **egg roll or spring roll skins (noodle type)**
1 **pound teleme or jack cheese**

Prepare Chicken-Prosciutto Filling and Creamy Tomato-Mint Sauce.

Mound ⅓ cup of the filling along a long edge of each egg roll skin (cover remaining noodles with plastic wrap); roll to enclose. Spread half the sauce in a shallow 9- by 13-inch baking dish. Place cannelloni, seam sides down, slightly apart in sauce. Spread with remaining sauce. Top each roll with a slice of cheese just slightly larger than top of roll. (At this point, you may cover and refrigerate for up to a day.) Transport in a cooler.

Bake, uncovered, in a 400° oven until lightly browned (30 to 40 minutes). Makes 6 servings.

*Chicken-Prosciutto Filling.* Coarsely chop 6 ounces thinly sliced **prosciutto** or ham; set aside. Remove and discard skin and bones from 1 **whole chicken breast** (1 to 1¼ lbs.). Cut meat into about ½-inch pieces and set aside.

In a wide frying pan, combine 1 large **onion,** finely chopped, and 2 tablespoons **butter** or margarine. Cook over medium heat, stirring often, until onion is soft. Add chicken and cook, stirring, until meat is no longer pink when slashed (about 3 minutes). Add prosciutto. Transfer mixture to a food processor and whirl until coarsely ground; or mince with a knife.

Mix in 2 **egg yolks,** ⅔ cup grated **Parmesan cheese,** 8 ounces **ricotta cheese,** and ⅛ to ¼ teaspoon **ground nutmeg.** Season to taste with **salt** and **white pepper.** If made ahead, cover and refrigerate for up to a day.

*Creamy Tomato-Mint Sauce.* Heat 3 tablespoons **olive oil** in a wide frying pan over medium heat. Add 2 medium-size **onions,** finely chopped, and 2 cloves **garlic,** minced or pressed. Cook, stirring often, until onions are soft but not browned. Add 1 large can (28 oz.) and 1 small can (14 oz.) **Italian-style tomatoes,** 1½ tablespoons **dry mint,** 1½ teaspoons **dry basil,** and 1 cup **regular-strength chicken broth.** With a spoon, break up tomatoes. Boil gently, uncovered, until sauce is slightly thickened and reduced to 6 cups (about 20 minutes).

Stir in ½ cup **whipping cream.** Season to taste with **salt** and **pepper.** If made ahead, cover and refrigerate for up to a day.

*Per serving: 888 calories, 55 g protein, 46 g carbohydrates, 54 g total fat, 297 mg cholesterol, 1575 mg sodium*

## Parmesan Dijon Chicken

*Pictured on page 30*

◆◆

*Preparation time: 10 minutes*

*Baking time: About 15 minutes*

A buttery coating of bread crumbs, cheese, mustard, and wine keeps these baked chicken breasts tender and moist.

2 or 3 **slices white bread**
1 **cup (about 5 oz.) grated Parmesan cheese**
⅓ **cup butter or margarine, melted**
⅔ **cup Dijon mustard**
3 **tablespoons dry white wine**
4 **whole chicken breasts (about 1 lb. *each*), skinned, boned, and split**
**Parsley sprigs**
**Lemon slice**

Tear bread into pieces. Whirl in a blender or food processor until coarse crumbs form. In a shallow pan, combine bread crumbs, cheese, and butter.

In another shallow pan, mix mustard and wine. Coat chicken with mustard mixture and then dip skinned side of each piece in crumb mixture. Arrange chicken, crumb sides up, slightly apart in a greased shallow rimmed baking pan. (At this point, you may cover and refrigerate for up to 8 hours.)

Bake, uncovered, in a 500° oven until chicken is golden brown and meat in thickest part is no longer pink when slashed (about 15 minutes). Transfer chicken to a warm platter. Insulate to transport hot (see page 5). To serve, garnish with parsley and lemon slice. Makes 8 servings.

*Per serving: 359 calories, 42 g protein, 8 g carbohydrates, 16 g total fat, 120 mg cholesterol, 1145 mg sodium*

# Baked Chicken Legs, Mexican-style

Preparation time: 20 minutes

Baking time: 40 to 45 minutes

A boldly seasoned coating envelops whole chicken legs. Serve with guacamole or a squeeze of lime juice.

2 eggs
⅓ cup bottled green chile salsa or taco sauce
¼ teaspoon salt
1¼ cups fine dry bread crumbs
1½ teaspoons *each* chili powder and ground cumin
1 teaspoon garlic salt
½ teaspoon dry oregano
6 to 8 whole chicken legs, thighs attached (3 to 3½ lbs. *total*)
6 tablespoons butter or margarine

In a shallow bowl, beat eggs, salsa, and salt until blended. In another shallow bowl, combine bread crumbs, chili powder, cumin, garlic salt, and oregano. Dip chicken into egg mixture and roll in crumb mixture; repeat both steps 1 more time.

In a shallow rimmed baking pan, melt butter as oven preheats to 400°. Remove pan from oven. Add chicken, turn to coat with butter, and arrange skin side up. Bake, uncovered, until meat near thigh-bone is no longer pink when slashed (40 to 45 minutes). Transfer chicken to a warm platter; insulate to transport hot (see page 5). Makes 6 to 8 servings.

*Per serving: 391 calories, 29 g protein, 13 g carbohydrates, 24 g total fat, 183 mg cholesterol, 668 mg sodium*

# Chicken, Rice & Tomatillo Bake

Preparation time: 40 minutes

Baking time: 45 to 55 minutes

Green chiles, cilantro, and tomatillos bake with plump chicken thighs and cumin-accented rice in this lively potluck offering.

12 chicken thighs (about 4 lbs. *total*)
2 tablespoons salad oil
1 large onion, finely chopped
2 cloves garlic, minced or pressed
2 teaspoons ground cumin
2 cups long-grain white rice
2 cans (13 oz. *each*) tomatillos
  About 2 cups regular-strength chicken broth
1 large can (7 oz.) whole green chiles, thinly sliced crosswise
¼ cup minced fresh cilantro (coriander)

Rinse chicken and pat dry. Heat oil in a wide frying pan over medium-high heat. Add chicken, a few pieces at a time (do not crowd), and cook until browned on all sides. Remove pieces as they brown and set aside. When all chicken is browned, pour off and discard all but 3 tablespoons of the drippings.

Reduce heat to medium and add onion, garlic, cumin, and rice to drippings in pan. Cook, stirring often, until rice is golden (about 5 minutes); set aside.

Drain liquid from tomatillos into a large measuring cup; add enough broth to make 4 cups. Cut tomatillos in half. In a shallow 4-quart casserole, combine liquid mixture, tomatillos, chiles, cilantro, and rice mixture; arrange chicken pieces, skin sides up, over rice.

Bake, uncovered, in a 350° oven until meat near thighbone is no longer pink when slashed, rice is tender, and liquid is absorbed (45 to 55 minutes). Insulate to transport hot (see page 5). Makes 12 servings.

*Per serving: 363 calories, 23 g protein, 30 g carbohydrates, 16 g total fat, 75 mg cholesterol, 437 mg sodium*

# Crispy Oven-fried Chicken for a Dozen

Preparation time: 20 minutes

Baking time: 50 to 55 minutes

Oven-frying takes much of the work out of cooking crisp and tender chicken for a crowd. For a moist and juicy result, dip the chicken pieces in buttermilk before coating with the seasoned cornmeal mixture.

3 **frying chickens (3 to 3½ lbs. *each*), cut up**
1¾ **cups all-purpose flour**
⅔ **cup yellow cornmeal**
1 **tablespoon chili powder**
2 **teaspoons seasoned salt**
1¼ **teaspoons *each* dry thyme and oregano**
½ **cup grated Parmesan cheese**
1½ **cups buttermilk**
12 **tablespoons (¼ lb. plus ¼ cup) butter or margarine**

Rinse chicken pieces and pat dry.

In a bag, combine flour, cornmeal, chili powder, seasoned salt, thyme, oregano, and cheese. Pour buttermilk into a shallow pan. Dip chicken pieces into buttermilk, drain briefly, and then shake, a few pieces at a time, in cornmeal mixture until evenly coated.

Line 2 rimmed 10- by 15-inch baking pans with heavy foil. Place half the butter in each pan. Set pans in a 400° oven just until butter is melted (2 to 3 minutes). Dip chicken pieces in melted butter to coat and arrange, skin sides down, in pans.

Bake, uncovered, for 25 minutes. Turn chicken and continue baking until pieces are browned and meat near thighbone is no longer pink when slashed (25 to 30 more minutes). Arrange on a rimmed platter. Insulate to transport hot (see page 5). Makes 12 servings.

*Per serving: 645 calories, 53 g protein, 22 g carbohydrates, 37 g total fat, 189 mg cholesterol, 565 mg sodium*

# Chicken, Chile & Cheese Casserole

◆

*Preparation time: 1 hour*

*Cooking time: 1 hour and 20 minutes*

*Baking time: About 1 hour; longer if refrigerated*

Mexican in inspiration and festive in appearance, this casserole, topped with garlic-seasoned cherry tomatoes, is also generous in capacity. Tempting menu partners might include a marinated green bean salad and, for dessert, Dark Chocolate Chewy Brownies (see page 90) with ice cream.

3 **frying chickens (3½ to 4 lbs. *each*)**
2 **cans (14½ oz. *each*) regular-strength chicken broth**
⅓ **cup *each* all-purpose flour and cold water, smoothly combined**
2 **tablespoons olive oil**
1 **large green bell pepper, seeded and finely chopped**
1 **large onion, finely chopped**
1 **can (4 oz.) whole green chiles, seeded and chopped**
2 **cloves garlic, minced or pressed**
4 **cups (1 lb.) shredded jack cheese**
1½ **cups sour cream**
**Cherry Tomato Topping (recipe follows)**

Rinse chickens (reserve giblets for other uses) and place in a 12-quart pan. Add broth and bring to a boil over high heat; reduce heat, cover, and simmer until drumsticks move easily when jiggled (about 1 hour). Lift chickens from broth and let cool.

Meanwhile, skim and discard fat from broth; boil broth, uncovered, over high heat until reduced to 1¼ cups. Remove from heat and gradually blend in flour and water mixture. Return to heat and bring to a boil. Cook, stirring constantly, until very thick (about 5 minutes); set aside.

Remove and discard chicken skin and bones; cut meat into large strips (you should have about 2 quarts).

Heat oil in an 8- to 10-inch frying pan over medium-high heat. Add bell pepper and onion. Cook, stirring, until vegetables are limp. Add to broth mixture along with chiles and garlic.

In a 9- by 13-inch baking pan or shallow casserole, layer half the chicken; top with half the sauce and sprinkle with half the cheese. Top with remaining chicken and sauce. Spread smoothly with sour cream and sprinkle with remaining cheese. (At this point, you may cover and refrigerate for up to a day.)

Bake, uncovered, in a 325° oven until hot (about 1 hour; 1¼ hours if refrigerated). Meanwhile, prepare Cherry Tomato Topping. Insulate casserole to transport hot (see page 5); transport topping separately.

Just before serving, spoon topping over casserole. Makes about 12 servings.

***Cherry Tomato Topping.*** Mix 2 cups **cherry tomatoes,** halved; ¼ teaspoon **garlic salt;** and 2 tablespoons *each* **olive oil** and **minced parsley.**

*Per serving: 657 calories, 60 g protein, 8 g carbohydrates, 42 g total fat, 179 mg cholesterol, 744 mg sodium*

# Turkey Eggplant Parmesan

*Pictured on facing page*

◼️

*Preparation time: 45 minutes*

*Baking time: 45 minutes to 1 hour*

Green chiles introduce a flavor surprise to classic eggplant parmigiana. Both ground turkey and eggplant that's oven browned rather than fried assure a lighter than usual result.

**Oven-browned Eggplant (recipe follows)**
2 tablespoons **olive oil**
1 pound **ground turkey, crumbled**
2 cloves **garlic, minced or pressed**
2 tablespoons **Italian herb seasoning** or 1½ teaspoons *each* **dry basil, oregano, thyme, and marjoram**
2 tablespoons **all-purpose flour**
1 can (4 oz.) **diced green chiles**
1 cup (about 5 oz.) **grated Parmesan cheese**
1 can (15 oz.) **tomato sauce**
¼ cup **chopped parsley**

Prepare Oven-browned Eggplant.

Meanwhile, heat oil in a wide frying pan over medium-high heat. Add turkey, garlic, and Italian herb seasoning. Cook, stirring occasionally, until most of the liquid has evaporated and turkey is lightly browned (about 10 minutes). Sprinkle flour over turkey and stir in along with chiles. Continue to cook, stirring constantly, until mixture looks dry (about 5 more minutes). Remove from heat and stir in half the cheese; set aside.

Arrange half the eggplant in a shallow 2- to 2½-quart casserole. Cover with half the turkey and half the tomato sauce. Repeat layers. Sprinkle with parsley and remaining cheese. (At this point, you may cover and refrigerate for up to 2 days.)

Bake, covered, in a 375° oven until hot (45 minutes to 1 hour). Insulate to transport hot (see page 5). Makes 6 servings.

***Oven-browned Eggplant.*** Slice 1 large **eggplant** (about 1¾ lbs.) ¼ inch thick. Using 3 to 4 tablespoons **olive oil,** brush with oil. Arrange in a single layer in a shallow rimmed baking pan. Bake, uncovered, in a 425° oven until browned (25 to 30 minutes), turning slices once, if necessary, to brown evenly. Season to taste with **salt** and **pepper.**

*Per serving: 428 calories, 26 g protein, 19 g carbohydrates, 28 g total fat, 69 mg cholesterol, 1078 mg sodium*

# Turkey Tonnato

◼️

*Preparation time: 15 minutes*

*Baking time: 1¼ to 2¼ hours*

*Chilling time: At least 4 hours*

A richly refreshing tuna and caper sauce adorns slices of cold roast turkey breast in this adaptation of an Italian summer classic. Good companions include a crisp green salad, a pasta salad, and crusty bread.

1 **boned, rolled, and tied turkey breast** (3½ to 5 lbs.)
1 small **onion, finely chopped**
½ cup **dry white wine**
2 tablespoons **butter** or **margarine, melted**
1 can (about 7 oz.) **tuna, drained**
2 tablespoons *each* **drained capers** and **lemon juice**
1 clove **garlic**
½ cup **mayonnaise** (optional)
3 or 4 **hard-cooked eggs, halved**
3 **medium-size tomatoes, cut into wedges**
**Watercress sprigs**

Place turkey, skin side up, in a shallow roasting pan (not on a rack); insert a meat thermometer in thickest part. In a small bowl, mix onion, wine, and butter; pour over turkey.

Roast, uncovered, in a 325° oven for 20 to 25 minutes per pound or until thermometer registers 165° (1¼ to 2¼ hours); baste several times with pan drippings.

Remove turkey from pan, reserving drippings. Let turkey cool; then cover and refrigerate for at least 4 hours or for up to 2 days.

Meanwhile, skim and discard fat from pan drippings. Scrape up browned bits and pour into a measuring cup. Add water, if needed, to make ½ cup. Whirl in a blender or food processor until smooth. Add tuna, capers, lemon juice, and garlic; whirl until puréed. Pour sauce into a bowl and blend in mayonnaise, if desired. Cover and refrigerate for at least 4 hours or for up to 2 days.

Discard strings and skin from turkey roast; slice meat thinly. Arrange on a platter. Garnish with eggs, tomatoes, and watercress. Transport turkey and sauce separately in a cooler. Offer sauce to add to taste. Makes 8 servings.

*Per serving: 342 calories, 59 g protein, 3 g carbohydrates, 9 g total fat, 283 mg cholesterol, 293 mg sodium*

### A Taste of Italy

*For an appetizer with gusto, choose Garden-fresh Bagna Cauda (page 16), a
garlicky dip served with raw vegetables. To follow, offer Turkey Eggplant Parmesan
(facing page), adapted from a popular Italian classic.*

## Steamed Turkey Breast with Herb Mayonnaise

*Preparation time: 15 minutes*

*Cooking time: 1 to 1½ hours*

*Chilling time: At least 4 hours*

Cold slices of turkey presented with a fresh herb mayonnaise and a selection of sourdough and whole grain breads—what potluck platter could be simpler or more enticing? The key to superb, moist meat is to steam the turkey breast gently before chilling it.

**1 whole or half turkey breast (3 to 4 lbs.)**
**6 parsley sprigs**
**1 small onion, thinly sliced**
**Green Herb Mayonnaise (recipe follows)**

Place turkey on a sheet of heavy foil large enough to enclose it; insert a meat thermometer into thickest part (not touching bone). Top turkey with parsley and onion; wrap in foil, shaping foil around thermometer. Place on a rack above 1 to 2 inches boiling water. Cover and steam (adding water, if necessary) for 20 to 25 minutes per pound or until thermometer registers 165° (1 to 1½ hours).

Meanwhile, prepare Green Herb Mayonnaise.

Remove turkey from pan, discarding parsley and onion. When cool enough to handle, remove and discard skin and bones. Cover and refrigerate for at least 4 hours or for up to 2 days. Slice turkey thinly and arrange on a platter. Transport turkey and mayonnaise separately in a cooler. Offer mayonnaise to add to taste. Makes 12 to 15 servings.

***Green Herb Mayonnaise.*** In a food processor, combine 1 cup lightly packed **watercress sprigs,** 1 cup lightly packed **parsley sprigs,** ⅓ cup sliced **green onions** (including tops), 1 clove **garlic,** and ¼ teaspoon **dry rosemary;** whirl until finely chopped. (Or finely chop watercress, parsley, green onions, and garlic; then add rosemary.) Blend in ½ cup **mayonnaise.** Cover and refrigerate for at least 30 minutes or for up to 2 days.

*Per serving turkey: 116 calories, 23 g protein, 0 g carbohydrate, 2 g total fat, 52 mg cholesterol, 51 mg sodium*

*Per tablespoon mayonnaise: 42 calories, .20 g protein, .54 g carbohydrate, 4 g total fat, 3 mg cholesterol, 34 mg sodium*

## Turkey & Mint-Avocado Pinwheels

*Pictured on page 54*

*Preparation time: 25 minutes*

*Standing and chilling time: About 1¼ hours*

Sliced into pinwheels, these sandwiches, rolled in rounds of softened Armenian cracker bread, reveal an appetizing filling of turkey, cucumber, cheese, and minted avocado spread. At a summer potluck, they'll disappear almost as fast as you serve them.

**2 pieces cracker bread (*each* 14 inches in diameter)**
**Mint-Avocado Spread (recipe follows)**
⅔ **cup slivered almonds**
**3 cups shredded cooked turkey**
1⅓ **cups thinly sliced cucumber**
⅓ **cup sliced ripe olives**
**2 cups (8 oz.) shredded jack cheese**

To soften cracker bread, hold each round under a gentle spray of cold water for about 10 seconds on each side or until well moistened. Stack rounds and place between clean, damp cloth towels. Let stand until soft and pliable (45 minutes to 1 hour). Check often; if rounds still seem crisp in spots, sprinkle with more water.

Meanwhile, prepare Mint-Avocado Spread.

Lay crackers side by side; spread half the avocado mixture on each cracker to within ½ inch of edges. Then top each with half each of the almonds, turkey, cucumber, olives, and cheese.

Roll each cracker up compactly, jelly roll style. Seal in plastic wrap and refrigerate for at least 30 minutes or for up to 2 hours. Transport in a cooler.

To serve, slice each roll into 1½-inch rounds. Makes 4 to 6 servings.

***Mint-Avocado Spread.*** Pit, peel, and mash 2 large softly ripe **avocados.** Blend in ¼ cup **lemon juice,** 3 tablespoons chopped **fresh mint** or 5 teaspoons crumbled dry mint, ½ teaspoon **pepper,** and ⅛ teaspoon **ground red pepper** (cayenne). Season to taste with **salt.**

*Per serving: 694 calories, 40 g protein, 48 g carbohydrates, 39 g total fat, 87 mg cholesterol, 569 mg sodium*

# Turkey & Chile Crêpes

*Preparation time: 25 minutes*

*Cooking time: 30 minutes*

*Baking time: 25 to 30 minutes*

Hot, spicy, and gilded with cheese, this casserole may remind you of enchiladas. Its turkey filling is appealingly light. For a colorful accompaniment, offer cherry tomatoes.

|  |  |
|---|---|
| 12 | to 14 Tender Crêpes (recipe follows) |
| 2 | tablespoons butter or margarine |
| 1 | pound ground turkey |
| 2 | cloves garlic, minced or pressed |
| 1 | large onion, finely chopped |
| 1 | teaspoon *each* ground cumin, salt, and chili powder |
| 1 | can (7 oz.) diced green chiles |
| ½ | cup sour cream |
| 1½ | cups (6 oz.) shredded jack cheese |
| 1 | cup (4 oz.) shredded Cheddar cheese |

Prepare Tender Crêpes and set aside.

In a wide frying pan, melt butter over medium-high heat. Crumble turkey into pan and cook, stirring often, until lightly browned. Mix in garlic, onion, cumin, salt, and chili powder. Cook, stirring often, until onion is soft but not browned. Remove from heat and stir in chiles, sour cream, and jack cheese.

Place about ⅓ cup of the filling down center of each crêpe. Roll up and place, seam sides down, in a single layer in two 9- by 13-inch baking dishes. Sprinkle with Cheddar cheese. (At this point, you may cover and refrigerate for up to a day.) Transport in a cooler. Bake, covered, in a 375° oven until hot (25 to 30 minutes). Makes 6 servings.

**Tender Crêpes.** In a blender or food processor, combine 2 **eggs,** ½ teaspoon **salt,** and 1 cup **all-purpose flour;** whirl until smooth. Blend in 1½ cups **milk** and 2 tablespoons **salad oil.**

Heat a 7- to 8-inch crêpe or other flat-bottomed frying pan over medium-high heat until a drop of water dances in pan. Add ½ teaspoon **butter** or margarine, tilting pan to coat bottom. Pour a scant ¼ cup of the batter all at once into center of pan, swiftly tilting pan so batter flows over entire surface.

Cook until lightly browned on bottom (30 to 40 seconds). Turn and cook until other side is browned (about 20 seconds). Let cool. Repeat to make additional crêpes, adding more butter as needed and stirring batter occasionally. Crêpes may be stacked. If made ahead, cover and refrigerate for up to 2 days. Bring to room temperature before separating. Makes 12 to 14 crêpes.

*Per serving: 580 calories, 33 g protein, 25 g carbohydrates, 39 g total fat, 214 mg cholesterol, 1198 mg sodium*

# Oregonian Turkey Chili

*Pictured on page 54*

*Preparation time: 15 minutes*

*Cooking time: 35 to 40 minutes*

Turkey is the surprise ingredient in this easily portable chili, making it lighter than usual, yet richly flavored. It's perfect for a picnic at the beach.

|  |  |
|---|---|
| 2 | large onions, finely chopped |
| 3 | tablespoons salad oil |
| 1 | cup chopped green bell pepper |
| 2 | cloves garlic, minced or pressed |
| 2 | pounds ground turkey |
| 1 | can (14½ oz.) tomatoes |
| 3 | cans (15 oz. *each*) kidney beans, drained |
| 2 | large cans (15 oz. *each*) tomato sauce |
| ¼ | cup soy sauce |
| 3 | tablespoons chili powder |
| 1 | teaspoon *each* ground cumin, dry sage, and dry thyme |
| 2 | limes, cut into wedges |

Set aside ½ cup of the onions for garnish.

Heat oil in a 6- to 8-quart pan over medium-high heat. Add bell pepper, garlic, and remaining onions. Cook, stirring often, until onions are soft.

Increase heat to high; crumble turkey into pan and cook, stirring gently, until drippings begin to brown. Add tomatoes (break up with a spoon) and their liquid, beans, tomato sauce, soy sauce, chili powder, cumin, sage, and thyme, stirring to scrape up browned bits. Reduce heat, cover, and simmer for 30 minutes. Insulate to transport hot (see page 5).

To serve, garnish with reserved onions and offer lime wedges to squeeze over chili to taste. Makes 6 to 8 servings.

*Per serving: 438 calories, 32 g protein, 42 g carbohydrates, 18 g total fat, 76 mg cholesterol, 1931 mg sodium*

**Variations on a Theme**

*For convenience—and great taste—try these versatile meat-and-vegetable dishes
(clockwise from top): Hungarian Cabbage Rolls stuffed with beef (page 72),
lamb-filled Molded Moussaka (page 82), and Pork Chops & Potatoes
au Gratin (page 80).*

# Meats

When selecting meat dishes to take to a potluck, look for those that adapt easily to transporting and don't require precise timing. You can count on delicious success with each of the recipes in this chapter. They include tempting entrées to enhance any menu, such as a substantial salad that features ham, ever-popular casseroles that combine meat with pasta or beans, and robust, vegetable-brightened stews. You can cook most of these dishes completely at home; insulate them well to keep them hot during the trip to the potluck.

## Three-layer Beef Casserole

*Preparation time: 45 minutes*

*Baking time: About 40 minutes; longer if refrigerated*

Green spinach pasta and golden Cheddar cheese join beef in this popular potluck casserole.

- 2 **pounds lean ground beef**
- 2 **cloves garlic, minced or pressed**
- 1 **large onion, finely chopped**
- 2 **large cans (15 oz. *each*) tomato sauce**
- 1 **tablespoon dry basil**
- 1 **package (8 to 10 oz.) spinach fettuccine**
- 1 **cup (4 oz.) shredded Cheddar cheese**
- 1 **large package (8 oz.) cream cheese, at room temperature**
- ½ **cup *each* milk and sour cream**

Crumble ground beef into a wide frying pan over medium heat; cook, stirring, until browned. Spoon off and discard any excess fat. Stir in garlic, onion, tomato sauce, and basil. Reduce heat, cover, and simmer for 30 minutes.

Meanwhile, in a 6- to 8-quart pan, cook pasta in 4 quarts boiling water just until tender to bite (about 8 minutes). Or cook according to package directions. Drain.

Spoon meat mixture into a shallow 3-quart casserole. Top evenly with pasta and sprinkle with Cheddar cheese. In a bowl, beat cream cheese, milk, and sour cream until smooth; spread over Cheddar cheese. (At this point, you may cover and refrigerate for up to a day.)

Bake, covered, in a 350° oven until hot (about 40 minutes; up to 1 hour if refrigerated). Insulate to transport hot (see page 5). Makes 6 to 8 servings.

*Per serving: 572 calories, 32 g protein, 32 g carbohydrates, 35 g total fat, 150 mg cholesterol, 895 mg sodium*

## Open-faced Tamale Pie

*Preparation time: About 1 hour*

*Baking time: 35 to 40 minutes*

Between PTA suppers and club luncheons, tamale pie has always had a full social calendar. Rediscover this savory Western classic, garnished with tomato, sour cream, and cilantro.

    Cornmeal Crust (recipe follows)
 2  tablespoons salad oil
 1  medium-size onion, finely chopped
 1  large can (7 oz.) diced green chiles
 1½ pounds lean ground beef
 1  tablespoon chili powder
 1  cup bottled mild green or red taco sauce
 3  cups (12 oz.) shredded Cheddar cheese
 1  avocado
    Condiments

Prepare Cornmeal Crust; set aside.

Pour oil into a wide frying pan over medium heat. When oil is hot, add onion and chiles; cook, stirring occasionally, until onion is soft but not browned (8 to 10 minutes). Lift out; set aside.

Crumble ground beef into pan and add chili powder; increase heat to high and cook, stirring, until meat is browned (about 10 minutes). Remove from heat; spoon off and discard any excess fat. Stir in onion mixture, ½ cup of the taco sauce, and 1½ cups of the cheese; spoon into crust. (At this point, you may cover and refrigerate for up to a day.)

Transport pie, remaining 1½ cups cheese, avocado, and condiments separately in a cooler.

Bake pie, uncovered, in a 350° oven until hot in center (30 to 35 minutes). Top with remaining cheese and continue baking until cheese is melted (about 5 more minutes). Meanwhile, pit, peel, and slice avocado. Garnish pie with avocado. Offer condiments and remaining ½ cup taco sauce to add to taste. Makes 6 servings.

***Cornmeal Crust.*** In a 3- to 4-quart pan, combine 1½ cups **yellow cornmeal,** 3½ cups **water,** ½ tea-spoon *each* **ground cumin** and **salt,** and ¼ teaspoon **ground red pepper** (cayenne). Bring to a boil over high heat, stirring constantly; reduce heat to medium and cook, stirring, until mixture is thick enough to leave a path for 2 seconds when spoon is drawn through it (8 to 9 minutes). Spread mixture evenly over bottom and 1 inch up sides of a shallow ungreased 3-quart casserole.

***Condiments.*** In separate bowls, place 1 large **firm-ripe tomato,** seeded and chopped; 1 cup **sour cream;** and about 1 cup **fresh cilantro** (coriander).

*Per serving: 738 calories, 39 g protein, 45 g carbohydrates, 45 g total fat, 128 mg cholesterol, 1424 mg sodium*

## Hungarian Cabbage Rolls
*Pictured on page 70*

*Preparation time: 35 minutes*

*Baking time: 1 to 1½ hours*

Bring a taste of the old country to your next potluck with these cabbage leaf bundles of spiced beef, baked in a hearty tomato-sauerkraut sauce.

 1  head green cabbage (about 2¼ lbs.), cored
 ¼  cup butter or margarine
 2  large onions, finely chopped
 1½ teaspoons ground allspice
 1  pound lean ground beef
 1  cup cooked pearl barley or rice
 1  egg, lightly beaten
 2  tablespoons all-purpose flour
    Salt and pepper
 1  can (1 lb.) sauerkraut, drained
 2  cans (8 oz. *each*) tomato sauce
 ¼  cup firmly packed brown sugar
    Sour cream (optional)

In a 6- to 8-quart pan, immerse cabbage in boiling water over high heat; boil, uncovered, until leaves are flexible enough to pull from head (10 to 15 minutes). Drain and let stand until cool enough to handle. Remove and set aside 12 large leaves; shred remaining leaves.

In a wide frying pan, melt 2 tablespoons of the butter over medium-high heat; stir in onions and allspice. Cook, stirring often, until onions are soft but not browned (8 to 10 minutes). Crumble ground beef into pan and add barley; remove pan from heat. Stir in egg and flour. Season to taste with salt and pepper.

Spoon about ¼ cup of the meat mixture onto base of each cabbage leaf; fold in sides and roll to enclose. Set aside.

In same frying pan, melt remaining 2 table-spoons butter over medium-high heat; add shred-ded cabbage and cook, stirring, until cabbage be-gins to brown. Stir in sauerkraut, tomato sauce, and brown sugar. Spoon sauerkraut mixture into a

9- by 13-inch baking pan; arrange cabbage rolls, smooth sides up, in sauce. (At this point, you may cover and refrigerate for up to a day.)

Bake, covered, in a 350° oven until meat is no longer pink in center when cut (1 to 1½ hours). Insulate to transport hot (see page 5). Offer sour cream, if desired, to add to taste. Makes 6 servings.

*Per serving: 447 calories, 20 g protein, 38 g carbohydrates, 25 g total fat, 123 mg cholesterol, 1029 mg sodium*

# Wine-simmered Beef Cubes

*Pictured on page 35*

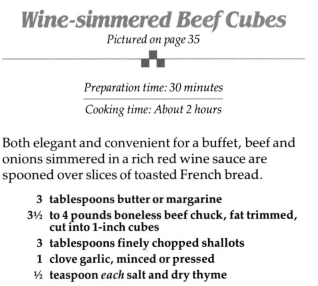

*Preparation time: 30 minutes*

*Cooking time: About 2 hours*

Both elegant and convenient for a buffet, beef and onions simmered in a rich red wine sauce are spooned over slices of toasted French bread.

- 3 tablespoons butter or margarine
- 3½ to 4 pounds boneless beef chuck, fat trimmed, cut into 1-inch cubes
- 3 tablespoons finely chopped shallots
- 1 clove garlic, minced or pressed
- ½ teaspoon *each* salt and dry thyme
- ¼ teaspoon pepper
- 2 cups dry red wine
- 12 to 15 boiling onions, peeled and cut in half lengthwise
- 1 tablespoon cornstarch blended with 2 tablespoons water
- 1 long loaf French bread, sliced, buttered, and toasted

In a 4½- to 5-quart pan, melt 1 tablespoon of the butter over medium-high heat. Add a third of the beef cubes; cook, turning beef, until browned on all sides. Remove from pan. Repeat with remaining butter and beef.

Return beef to pan; add shallots and garlic and cook, stirring, for 1 minute. Stir in salt, thyme, pepper, and wine. Increase heat to high and bring to a boil; reduce heat, cover, and simmer for 1 hour. Add onions (on top of mixture); cover and continue to cook until onions and beef are tender when pierced (about 30 minutes). Remove from heat. (At this point, you may cool, cover, and refrigerate for up to a day.)

Skim and discard fat. (Reheat if refrigerated.) With a slotted spoon, transfer meat and onions to a warm serving dish. Boil sauce, if necessary,

until reduced to 1¼ cups. Blend in cornstarch mixture. Cook, stirring, over medium-high heat until thickened and clear; pour over meat and onions. Insulate to transport hot (see page 5).

To serve, spoon portions over toasted bread slices. Makes 6 to 8 servings.

*Per serving: 309 calories, 30 g protein, 4 g carbohydrates, 19 g total fat, 110 mg cholesterol, 301 mg sodium*

# Apple Cider Stew

*Preparation time: 25 minutes*

*Cooking time: About 3 hours*

Apples thicken the spiced cider that enriches this beef and sweet potatoes stew.

- 4 pounds boneless beef stew meat, cut into 2-inch cubes
  About 3 cups apple cider
- 2 tart apples
- 1 cinnamon stick (about 2 inches long)
- 2 tablespoons cider vinegar
- 15 small onions (*each* about 1½ inches in diameter)
- 3 sweet potatoes (about 2 lbs. *total*), peeled and cut into 2-inch chunks
  Parsley sprigs

In a 5- to 6-quart pan, combine meat and ½ cup of the apple cider. Cover and place over medium heat to sweat out meat juices (about 30 minutes). Uncover and continue to cook until juices thicken, turning meat as needed until well browned on all sides (about 1 more hour).

Lift out meat; skim and discard fat. Peel, core, and chop apples; add to pan with cinnamon stick, vinegar, and 1½ more cups apple cider, stirring to scrape up browned bits. Return meat to pan and add onions and sweet potatoes. Reduce heat, cover, and simmer until meat is very tender (about 1½ hours); add more cider if mixture becomes too thick. (At this point, you may cover and refrigerate for up to a day.)

Skim and discard fat, if necessary. (Reheat if refrigerated.) Insulate to transport hot (see page 5). Garnish with parsley. Makes 6 to 8 servings.

*Per serving: 781 calories, 42 g protein, 38 g carbohydrates, 50 g total fat, 165 mg cholesterol, 115 mg sodium*

## Machaca Burritos

*Pictured on facing page*

◼︎◼︎

Preparation time: 15 minutes

Cooking time: 2 to 4 hours

Familiar to lovers of Mexican cuisine, *machaca*, or shredded cooked beef, makes a magnificent burrito. The meat takes at least 2 hours of gentle simmering to become easy to shred.

2½  to 3 pounds boneless beef chuck, fat trimmed, cut into ½-inch cubes
1  can (about 15 oz.) kidney beans
1  large green bell pepper, seeded and cut into thin strips
1  large can (7 oz.) diced green chiles
1  large onion, finely chopped
2  tablespoons chili powder
¾  teaspoon *each* salt and pepper
1  teaspoon *each* ground cumin and garlic powder
1  large tomato, chopped
20  to 24 small flour tortillas
    Condiments (suggestions follow)

Place beef in a heavy 4- to 5-quart pan or electric slow cooker. Add kidney beans and their liquid, bell pepper, chiles, and onion. Stir in chili powder, salt, pepper, cumin, garlic powder, and tomato. Cover and simmer, stirring occasionally, until meat shreds readily (about 2 hours). Or set slow cooker at low and cook for about 4 hours. If mixture is soupy, uncover during last part of cooking.

With wet hands, lightly dampen each tortilla. Stack and wrap in foil; heat in a 350° oven until warm (about 10 minutes). Insulate meat mixture and tortillas to transport hot (see page 5). Transport desired condiments separately in a cooler.

To serve, spoon filling down center of each tortilla; add condiments to taste. Roll or fold to enclose. Makes 10 to 12 servings.

**Condiments.** Serve two or more of the following: 2 cups (8 oz.) shredded **Cheddar cheese** or jack cheese, about 1 cup bottled **green chile salsa**, ¾ to 1 cup thinly sliced **green onions** (including tops), and about 1 cup **fresh cilantro** (coriander).

*Per serving: 308 calories, 20 g protein, 33 g carbohydrates, 11 g total fat, 47 mg cholesterol, 711 mg sodium*

## Oven-simmered Chile Short Ribs

◼︎◼︎

Preparation time: 15 minutes

Baking time: About 2½ hours

Cumin-seasoned rice, dotted with peas, makes a flavorful accompaniment to juicy beef short ribs.

4  to 5 pounds lean beef short ribs, cut into 2- to 3-inch lengths
1  large onion, cut into 8 to 10 wedges
2  tablespoons seeded and finely chopped fresh or canned hot chiles, such as jalapeño, Fresno, or serrano
2  cloves garlic, minced or pressed
1  cup catsup or tomato-base chili sauce
1  cup water
1  tablespoon *each* dry mustard and red wine vinegar
2  tablespoons brown sugar
    Cumin Rice with Peas (recipe follows)

Place short ribs in a 4- to 5-quart casserole; tuck onion around meat. In a bowl, mix chiles, garlic, catsup, water, mustard, vinegar, and brown sugar; pour over short ribs. Cover tightly and bake in a 425° oven, stirring occasionally, until meat is very tender when pierced and pulls away from bone easily (about 2½ hours). Remove from oven. (At this point, you may cool, cover, and refrigerate for up to a day.)

Skim and discard fat. (Reheat, covered, in a 375° oven for about 45 minutes if refrigerated.) Prepare Cumin Rice with Peas.

Meanwhile, with a slotted spoon, transfer ribs to a warm serving bowl. Boil sauce, if necessary, until reduced to about ¾ cup; spoon over meat. Insulate meat and rice to transport hot (see page 5). Makes 6 servings.

***Cumin Rice with Peas.*** In a 2- to 2½-quart pan, combine 2 cups **water,** 1 **beef bouillon cube,** and ½ teaspoon **ground cumin;** bring to a boil over high heat. Stir in 1 cup **long-grain white rice;** reduce heat, cover, and simmer until liquid is absorbed and rice is tender to bite (about 20 minutes). Stir in 1 package (10 oz.) or 2 cups **frozen tiny peas.** Cover and cook for about 2 more minutes. Transfer to a warm casserole and cover.

*Per serving: 480 calories, 32 g protein, 51 g carbohydrates, 16 g total fat, 76 mg cholesterol, 741 mg sodium*

### Bienvenidos a Mi Casa

*At a casual stand-up buffet, feature Mexico's robust Machaca Burritos made*
*with shredded beef (facing page) and piquant Sweet Corn Coblets (page 33).*
*Both are fun to eat out of hand.*

# Lasagne for a Crowd

Need an ace in the hole for hungry teenagers, school potlucks, or neighborhood block parties? You can rely on this lasagne to provide 50 to 60 delicious portions. Or, by using small pans, you can divide the mixture into portions that feed as few as 6 and freeze the remaining portions. Choose pan sizes and amounts of ingredients per pan from the chart on the facing page.

To add to the convenience of this recipe, its noodles don't require precooking. The sauce alone is enough to moisten and tenderize them as the lasagne bakes. You can either bake this dish while still frozen or let it thaw in the refrigerator and bake as if freshly made.

If you're serving the lasagne as a main dish at a dinner for 50 to 60 people, accompany it with garlic-buttered French bread and a green salad. Plan on about 6 loaves of bread to serve everyone.

The dressing and salad greens can be prepared ahead; just before serving, divide the greens into several large salad bowls and lightly mix in the dressing.

## Potluck Lasagne

Tomato Pork Sauce (recipe follows)

Sausage Meat Loaf (recipe follows)

2½  to 3 pounds lasagne noodles

5  pounds ricotta cheese

2½  pounds mozzarella cheese, thinly sliced

5  cups (about 1¼ lbs.) grated Parmesan cheese

Prepare Tomato Pork Sauce and Sausage Meat Loaf.

Rinse noodles under warm water to moisten and remove excess flour.

*To assemble each 9- by 13-inch pan,* refer to chart for quantities of ingredients to use. Spread 1 cup of the sauce in pan and cover with half the lasagne in a single layer. Layer with 1 cup more sauce, half the sausage mixture, and half each of the ricotta and mozzarella. Repeat layers one more time. Top with remaining 1 cup sauce and sprinkle with Parmesan cheese.

*To assemble each 9- by 13-inch pan,* refer to chart for quantities of ingredients to use. Spread 1 cup of the sauce in pan and cover with half the lasagne in a single layer. Layer with 1 cup more sauce, half the sausage mixture, and half each of the ricotta and mozzarella. Repeat layers one more time. Top with remaining 2 cups sauce and sprinkle with Parmesan cheese.

*To assemble each 11½- by 17-inch pan,* refer to chart for quantities of ingredients to use. Spread 1½ cups of the sauce in pan and cover with half the lasagne in a single layer. Layer with 1½ cups more sauce, half the sausage mixture, and half each of the ricotta and mozzarella. Repeat layers one more time. Top with remaining 4 cups sauce and sprinkle with Parmesan cheese.

If lasagne is prepared ahead, cover and refrigerate for up to 2 days or wrap and freeze for up to 2 months.

Bake, covered, following directions in chart, until hot in center. Uncover and continue baking until cheese is browned (about 8 to 10 more minutes). Makes 50 to 60 servings.

**Tomato Pork Sauce.** Trim excess fat from a 3½- to 4-pound boneless **pork butt** or shoulder roast; cut into 2-inch cubes.

In a 10- to 12-quart kettle, cook pork, covered, over medium-high heat to release juices (about 30 minutes). Uncover and increase heat to high. Cook, stirring occasionally, until meat is well browned (7 to 8 more minutes). Lift out meat and set aside.

Reduce heat to medium. Add 3 medium-size **onions,** coarsely chopped. Cover and cook for 3 to 4 minutes. Add 8 cloves **garlic,** minced or pressed, and cook, stirring, until onions are soft (about 10 more minutes).

Pour in ¼ cup **water,** stirring to scrape up browned bits. Add 6 large cans (28 oz. *each*) **pear-shaped tomatoes** and their liquid; break up tomatoes with a spoon. Stir in pork and 4 large cans (12 oz. *each*) **tomato paste.** Reduce heat, cover, and simmer until pork shreds easily (about 4 hours). You should have about 7½ quarts. Let cool.

Lift out meat and shred with fingers or 2 forks; return to sauce. (At this point, you may cover and refrigerate for up to 2 days.)

*Sausage Meat Loaf.* In a 10- to 12-quart bowl, mix 4 pounds *each* **lean ground beef** and **ground pork;** 8 **eggs;** 1 cup *each* finely chopped **parsley, grated Parmesan cheese,** and **fine dry bread crumbs;** 2 tablespoons *each* **fennel seeds** and **dry oregano;** 1 tablespoon **pepper;** 2 teaspoons **salt;** and 2 teaspoons **crushed red pepper.**

Divide meat mixture in half and pat each portion evenly into a shallow 10- by 15-inch rimmed baking pan. Bake, uncovered, in a 450° oven until tops are well browned (about 30 minutes). Let cool. (At this point, you may cover and refrigerate for up to 2 days.)

Chop meat mixture into about ½-inch chunks and mix with any juices.

*Per serving lasagne: 487 calories, 33 g protein, 27 g carbohydrates, 27 g total fat, 134 mg cholesterol, 780 mg sodium*

# Green Salad with Garlic Cream Dressing

½ cup **red wine vinegar**
3 tablespoons **Dijon mustard**
1 **egg**
3 cloves **garlic**
⅛ teaspoon **liquid hot pepper seasoning**
1½ teaspoons **sugar**
1 cup **salad oil**
½ cup **olive oil**
**Freshly ground black pepper**
2 heads **iceberg lettuce, washed and crisped**
2 bunches *each* **romaine and red leaf lettuce, washed and crisped**

In a blender or food processor, whirl vinegar, mustard, egg, garlic, liquid hot pepper seasoning, and sugar until garlic is puréed. With motor running, gradually add salad oil and olive oil in a thin steady stream until smoothly blended; season to taste with pepper. (At this point, you may cover and refrigerate for up to 2 weeks.)

Tear lettuce into bite-size pieces; mix lightly. Transport in a cooler.

To serve, arrange lettuce in serving bowls. Stir dressing, pour over salads, and mix lightly. Makes 50 to 60 servings.

*Per serving: 59 calories, .72 g protein, 2 g carbohydrates, 6 g total fat, 5 mg cholesterol, 28 mg sodium*

## Pans, Proportions & Baking Times

| Pan size | 9 by 9 pan | 9 by 13 pan | 11½ by 17 pan |
|---|---|---|---|
| Number of pans | 10 | 5 | 3 |
| Servings per pan | 6 | 10 to 12 | 16 to 20 |
| Cups of sauce per pan | 3 | 6 | 10 |
| Pounds of lasagne noodles per pan | ¼ | ½ | 1 |
| Amount of sausage mixture per pan | About 2½ cups | About 4½ cups | About 8 cups |
| Pounds of ricotta cheese per pan | ½ | 1 | 1⅔ |
| Pounds of mozzarella cheese per pan | ¼ | ½ | ¾ |
| Cups of Parmesan cheese per pan | ½ | 1 | 1⅔ |
| Baking time (350°) | 45 minutes | 1 hour | 2 hours |
| Baking time if frozen (325°) | 3 hours | 3 hours | 4 hours |

**French Impressions**

*Easily portable to a potluck, Black Bean Cassoulet (facing page), adapted from a classic
French casserole, needs only the simple accompaniment of juicy sliced tomatoes.
For dessert, present another inspiration from France, Almond Toffee Tart (page 92).*

## Black Bean Cassoulet

*Pictured on facing page*

■■
■

*Preparation time: 3 hours*

*Baking time: About 1 hour*

Originally from southwestern France, where it's made with white beans and duck, cassoulet travels to the American Southwest. Now it boasts black beans, chicken, pork, and bold seasonings.

- 3 large onions
- ¼ pound sliced bacon, chopped
- 2 tablespoons coarsely chopped fresh ginger
- 1 fresh jalapeño chile, seeded and finely chopped
- 1½ tablespoons dry oregano
- 1 tablespoon *each* dry thyme and cumin seeds
- 4 cloves garlic, minced or pressed
- 1½ pounds black beans
- 2 pounds boneless pork shoulder or butt, fat trimmed, cut into 1-inch chunks
- About 7 cups regular-strength chicken broth
- 10 chicken thighs (3 to 3½ lbs. *total*)
- 1 pound mild Italian sausages
- ¼ cup butter or margarine
- 1 cup coarse soft bread crumbs
- ¼ cup chopped fresh cilantro (coriander)

Coarsely chop half of one of the onions. In a 7- to 8-quart pan, cook chopped onion and bacon, stirring, over medium heat until onion is golden (10 to 15 minutes). Add ginger, chile, oregano, thyme, cumin, and half the garlic; cook, stirring, until garlic is soft (about 2 minutes).

Sort beans and discard any debris. Rinse well and drain. Add beans and pork to onion mixture; cover with about 6 cups of the broth. Bring to a boil; reduce heat, cover, and simmer, stirring occasionally, until beans mash easily (about 2½ hours).

Meanwhile, place remaining onions (unpeeled) in a shallow baking pan. Bake, uncovered, in a 350° oven until soft (about 1½ hours). Let cool; peel and cut lengthwise into quarters.

At same time, arrange chicken, skin sides up, and sausages in a single layer in a shallow 10- by 15-inch rimmed baking pan. Bake, uncovered, in a 350° oven until meat near bone is no longer pink when slashed (about 40 minutes). Cut sausages into ⅜-inch-thick diagonal slices.

In a medium-size frying pan, melt butter over medium-high heat. Add bread crumbs and remaining garlic. Cook, stirring, until crumbs are light brown (about 3 minutes). Set aside. Turn bean mixture into a 6- to 7-quart casserole. Mix in onions, chicken, and sausages. (At this point, you may cover and refrigerate cassoulet and crumbs separately for up to 3 days; before baking, add 1 more cup broth to cold cassoulet.)

Sprinkle cassoulet with crumbs. Bake, uncovered, in a 350° oven until hot in center (about 1 hour). Insulate to transport hot (see page 5).

To serve, garnish with cilantro. Makes 10 to 12 servings.

*Per serving: 743 calories, 48 g protein, 43 g carbohydrates, 42 g total fat, 161 mg cholesterol, 1103 mg sodium*

## Slow-cooked Ribs & Beans

■■
■

*Preparation time: 10 minutes*

*Soaking time: 8 hours*

*Cooking time: 8 to 12 hours in a slow cooker; 2 to 2½ hours on range*

Call it a stew or a knife-and-fork soup. Either way, this zesty combination is sure to please.

- 1 pound Great Northern beans
- 1 can (8 oz.) pineapple chunks
- 1 clove garlic, minced or pressed
- ½ cup soy sauce
- ¼ cup lemon juice
- 3 tablespoons molasses or honey
- 2 teaspoons chili powder
- 1 teaspoon *each* ground cumin and ginger
- ½ teaspoon pepper
- 2½ pounds country-style spareribs

Sort beans and discard any debris; rinse well and drain. Cover with water and let stand for 8 hours.

Drain beans and place in a 6-quart electric slow cooker or a 6-quart pan. Add 2½ cups water. Drain juice from pineapple chunks into beans; set pineapple aside. To beans add garlic, soy sauce, lemon juice, molasses, chili powder, cumin, ginger, pepper, and spareribs. If using cooker, cover and cook at low setting until beans and meat are tender (8 to 12 hours). If using pan, cover and bring to a boil; reduce heat and simmer until tender (2 to 2½ hours).

Skim and discard fat. Add pineapple chunks and cook until hot (5 to 10 minutes). Insulate to transport hot (see page 5). Makes 8 servings.

*Per serving: 441 calories, 24 g protein, 48 g carbohydrates, 18 g total fat, 49 mg cholesterol, 1080 mg sodium*

# Pork Picadillo

Preparation time: 10 minutes

Cooking time: About 1 hour and 20 minutes

Though it translates literally as "hash," Mexico's cinnamon-spiced *picadillo* actually makes a gala presentation with its toppings of avocado and lime. If you wish, you can spoon servings into warm tortillas to eat as soft tacos.

- 2 tablespoons *each* butter and salad oil
- 1 large onion, finely chopped
- 3½ pounds boneless pork shoulder, fat trimmed, cut into ¾-inch cubes
- 2 cloves garlic, minced or pressed
- 2 cans (8 oz. *each*) tomato sauce
- ½ cup tomato-base chili sauce
- 1 teaspoon ground cinnamon
- 1½ teaspoons salt
- ¼ teaspoon ground cumin
- ½ cup dried currants
- 3 tablespoons *each* brown sugar and red wine vinegar
- 2 green onions (including tops), thinly sliced
- 2 avocados
- 2 limes, cut into wedges

Heat 1 tablespoon each of the butter and oil in a 5- to 6-quart pan over medium-high heat. Add onion and cook, stirring often, until soft (8 to 10 minutes). Lift out with a slotted spoon and set aside.

Add remaining 1 tablespoon each butter and oil to pan. Add pork, about half at a time, and cook, turning, until browned. Return all meat and onion to pan and add garlic, tomato sauce, chili sauce, cinnamon, salt, cumin, currants, brown sugar, and vinegar. Reduce heat, cover, and simmer until meat is very tender when pierced (about 50 minutes); stir occasionally as meat cooks, adding a little water if sauce becomes too thick. (At this point, you may cool, cover, and refrigerate for up to 2 days; reheat, covered, in a 350° oven until hot, about 50 minutes.)

Transfer pork to a warm casserole. Insulate to transport hot (see page 5).

To serve, garnish with green onions. Pit, peel, and dice avocados. Offer avocados and lime wedges to add to taste. Makes 8 to 10 servings.

*Per serving: 378 calories, 27 g protein, 22 g carbohydrates, 21 g total fat, 90 mg cholesterol, 912 mg sodium*

# Pork Chops & Potatoes au Gratin

Pictured on page 70

Preparation time: 10 minutes

Cooking time: 45 to 50 minutes

Braised pork chops topped with a creamy sauce share a baking dish with cheese-gilded sliced potatoes.

- 2 pounds pork loin or shoulder chops (about ½ inch thick)
- ¾ cup *each* dry white wine and regular-strength beef broth
- 4 medium-size thin-skinned potatoes (about 2 lbs. *total*), peeled and sliced ¼ inch thick
- ½ cup whipping cream
- ¼ cup butter or margarine
- ⅛ teaspoon ground nutmeg
- 1 cup (4 oz.) shredded Swiss cheese
  Watercress sprigs

Place pork chops in a single layer in a wide frying pan. Cover and cook over medium heat for 5 minutes; uncover and cook, turning once, until juices have evaporated and meat is well browned on both sides. Remove chops from pan and set aside.

Add wine and broth to pan, stirring to scrape up browned bits. Evenly layer potatoes in pan and top with chops. Cover and simmer until potatoes are tender (about 25 minutes).

Lift out chops and arrange at one end of a shallow 10- to 12-inch oval heatproof casserole; arrange potatoes at opposite end. Keep warm.

Add cream to pan, increase heat to high, and boil, stirring, until sauce is reduced by about half. Reduce heat to low and add butter and nutmeg; stir until well blended. Insulate casserole and sauce separately to transport hot (see page 5).

Just before serving, sprinkle cheese over potatoes. Broil 4 to 5 inches below heat just until cheese is melted and begins to brown (2 to 3 minutes). Spoon sauce over chops and garnish with watercress. Makes 6 servings.

*Per serving: 632 calories, 31 g protein, 22 g carbohydrates, 46 g total fat, 147 mg cholesterol, 315 mg sodium*

## Mostaccioli & Swiss Cheese Casserole

◼◼

*Preparation time: 30 minutes*

*Baking time: About 30 minutes; longer if refrigerated*

In this version of macaroni and cheese, mostaccioli—a pasta whimsically named "little mustaches"—mingles with Swiss cheese, spinach, and slivered ham in a mustardy sauce.

- 8 ounces mostaccioli (penne)
- ¼ cup butter or margarine
- ¼ cup all-purpose flour
- 2 cups milk
- ¼ teaspoon liquid hot pepper seasoning
- 1 tablespoon Dijon mustard
- 3 cups (12 oz.) shredded Swiss cheese
- ½ pound cooked ham, cut into thin, bite-size slivers
- 1 package (10 oz.) frozen spinach, thawed
  Salt and pepper

In a 5- to 6-quart pan, cook pasta in 3 to 4 quarts boiling water just until tender to bite (10 to 12 minutes). Or cook according to package directions. Drain, rinse, and drain again; set aside.

In same pan, melt butter over medium heat; stir in flour and cook until bubbly. Remove from heat and gradually blend in milk. Increase heat to medium-high and cook, stirring constantly, until mixture comes to a boil. Add hot pepper seasoning, mustard, and 2 cups of the cheese, stirring until cheese is melted. Remove from heat.

Add pasta and ham to sauce; mix gently.

Squeeze as much liquid as possible from spinach; stir into pasta mixture. Spread in a shallow 2-quart casserole. (At this point, you may cover and refrigerate for up to a day.) Transport in a cooler.

Bake, covered, in a 350° oven for 20 minutes (30 minutes if refrigerated). Uncover, sprinkle with remaining 1 cup cheese, and continue baking until cheese is melted and mixture is bubbly (about 10 more minutes). Season to taste with salt and pepper. Makes 6 servings.

*Per serving: 571 calories, 34 g protein, 40 g carbohydrates, 30 g total fat, 107 mg cholesterol, 949 mg sodium*

## Crunchy Rice, Bean & Ham Salad

◼◼

*Preparation time: 15 minutes*

*Chilling time: At least 8 hours*

Poured on hot, the sweet-sour dressing for this colorful main-course salad imparts piquant flavor to the ingredients as they chill.

- Sweet-Sour Dressing (recipe follows)
- 3 cups cooked long-grain white rice
- 1 can (about 15 oz.) kidney beans, drained
- 1½ cups thinly sliced celery
- ½ cup *each* thinly sliced green onions (including tops) and seeded, chopped green bell pepper
- 1 jar (2 oz.) sliced pimentos, drained
- 8 ounces cooked ham, cut into thin strips (about 2 cups *total*)
  Romaine lettuce leaves, washed and crisped
- 2 medium-size tomatoes, cut into wedges
- 2 hard-cooked eggs, sliced

Prepare Sweet-Sour Dressing.

In a large bowl, combine rice, beans, celery, green onions, bell pepper, pimentos, and ham. Pour hot dressing over rice mixture; stir lightly. Cover and refrigerate, stirring occasionally, for at least 8 hours or for up to a day.

Line a bowl or deep platter with lettuce; fill with rice salad. Garnish with tomatoes and eggs. Transport in a cooler. Makes 6 to 8 servings.

*Sweet-Sour Dressing.* In a small pan, combine ⅓ cup **cider vinegar**, 3 tablespoons **sugar**, ¼ cup **salad oil**, 2 tablespoons **Dijon mustard**, 2 teaspoons **garlic salt**, 1 teaspoon **pepper**, and ¼ teaspoon **liquid hot pepper seasoning**. Bring to a boil over high heat, stirring until sugar is dissolved. Keep warm over lowest heat.

*Per serving: 302 calories, 11 g protein, 36 g carbohydrates, 12 g total fat, 80 mg cholesterol, 1161 mg sodium*

## Italian Meat & Cheese Turnover

*Preparation time: 20 minutes*

*Baking time: 25 to 35 minutes*

When squadrons of salads dominate the potluck table, this giant turnover makes an appetizing addition.

½ pound *each* **thinly sliced cooked ham, cooked turkey, and salami**
8 ounces **ricotta cheese**
1 **egg**
2 teaspoons **Italian herb seasoning** or ½ teaspoon *each* **dry basil, oregano, thyme, and marjoram**
1½ cups (6 oz.) **shredded provolone cheese**
¼ cup **thinly sliced green onions (including tops)**
1 loaf (1 lb.) **frozen bread dough, thawed**
1 tablespoon **salad oil**

Cut meats into bite-size strips ¼ inch wide. In a large bowl, combine ricotta, egg, and Italian herb seasoning; mix well. Stir in meats, provolone cheese, and green onions.

On a lightly floured board, roll bread dough out into a 14-inch-diameter circle. Transfer to a large greased baking sheet. Mound cheese mixture over half the circle; fold dough over to cover filling. Moisten edges with water, fold over, and crimp to seal. With a fork, pierce dough in several places; brush with oil. (At this point, you may cover and refrigerate for up to 4 hours.)

Bake, uncovered, in a 350° oven until golden brown (25 to 35 minutes). Insulate to transport hot (see page 5). To serve, cut into thick slices. Makes 8 to 10 servings.

*Per serving: 321 calories, 19 g protein, 24 g carbohydrates, 16 g total fat, 73 mg cholesterol, 796 mg sodium*

## Molded Moussaka

*Pictured on page 70*

*Preparation time: About 1 hour*

*Baking time: About 45 minutes; longer if refrigerated*

Like a glossy purple cloak, the skins of hollowed-out eggplants envelop a filling of ground lamb, bell pepper, eggplant, fresh mint, and yogurt.

2 medium-size **eggplants (about 1 lb. *each*)**
**Olive oil or salad oil**
**Lamb and Mint Filling (recipe follows)**
**Lemon slices**
**Mint sprigs**
2 cups **plain yogurt (optional)**

Cut eggplants (unpeeled) lengthwise into quarters. With a curved knife, cut out pulp, leaving about ¼-inch-thick shells. Set pulp aside for filling.

Lightly rub skins with oil. Arrange shells, skin sides up, on a large oiled baking sheet. Bake, uncovered, in a 400° oven until skins feel very soft when pressed (30 to 45 minutes). Loosen from pan and let cool slightly.

Meanwhile, prepare Lamb and Mint Filling.

Arrange baked shells, skin sides down, in an oiled 9-inch round cake pan so they radiate out from center. Spoon filling evenly over shells; fold ends over filling. (At this point, you may cover and refrigerate for up to a day.)

Set pan on a rimmed baking sheet. Bake, uncovered, in a 400° oven until thoroughly hot in center (about 45 minutes; 55 minutes if refrigerated). Cover cake pan with a serving dish; holding dish and pan securely, invert and shake to loosen moussaka from pan. Insulate to transport hot (see page 5).

Serve hot or at room temperature, garnished with lemon slices and mint sprigs. Cut into wedges to serve. Offer yogurt to add to taste, if desired. Makes 8 servings.

***Lamb and Mint Filling.*** Heat ¼ cup **olive oil** or salad oil in a wide frying pan over medium heat. Add 2 large **onions,** finely chopped, and **reserved pulp** from eggplants, finely chopped. Cover and cook, stirring often, until eggplant mashes easily (20 to 25 minutes).

Add 3 cloves **garlic,** minced or pressed; 1½ pounds **lean ground lamb,** crumbled; and ¼ teaspoon **pepper.** Increase heat to high and cook, stirring often, until lamb is browned and juices have evaporated (12 to 15 minutes). Blend in 3 tablespoons **all-purpose flour;** 1 large **green bell pepper,** seeded and finely chopped; ½ cup finely chopped **fresh mint leaves;** and ¾ cup **plain yogurt.** Cook, stirring, until bubbly. Remove from heat and stir in 3 tablespoons **lemon juice.** Season to taste with **salt.**

*Per serving: 403 calories, 16 g protein, 15 g carbohydrates, 31 g total fat, 62 mg cholesterol, 68 mg sodium*

**Soup from the Garden**

*Bring your own freshly picked eggplant, beans, or other garden crop to add
to a convivial pot of Harvest Soup (page 84). Offer it with sliced Whole Wheat
Country Loaf (page 29).*

# Harvest Soup Party

An overabundant vegetable garden can create a lot of work at harvest time. Or, it can call for celebrating by throwing a potluck party. For this occasion, instead of casseroles, guests contribute zucchini, bok choy, corn, or other bounty from their gardens.

The host provides a bubbling broth into which goes a sampling of the vegetables brought by guests (afterwards, everyone can exchange any produce that doesn't go into the pot). With the stock prepared in advance, the soup will take only about half an hour. Add slowest-cooking vegetables first.

Pass sour cream, Parmesan cheese, and lemon wedges to season individual portions. As a hearty accompaniment, offer one of the easy breads on page 29. For dessert, set out Fruit Crisp (page 92), made with peaches, pears, or apples.

## Harvest Soup

Pictured on page 83

3 large cans (47 oz.) regular-strength chicken broth or 18 cups homemade chicken broth

3 pounds smoked ham hocks, cut into 1-inch-thick slices

2 large slices (about 2 lbs. *total*) meaty beef shanks (*each* about 1½ inches thick)

2 large onions, finely chopped

4 to 5 quarts vegetables, prepared as necessary and cut into bite-size pieces (suggestions follow)
Salt
Sour cream
Shredded Parmesan cheese
Lemon wedges

In a large (at least 10-quart size) kettle, combine broth, ham hocks, beef shanks, and onions. Bring to a boil over medium-high heat. Reduce heat, cover, and

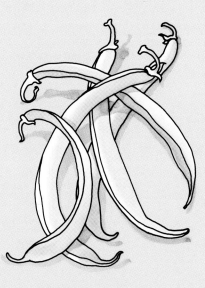

simmer until meat is very tender when pierced (about 2 hours). Lift out meat and discard bones, fat, and skin. Cut meat into bite-size pieces and return to broth. (At this point, you may cool, cover, and refrigerate for up to a day.)

Skim and discard fat. (Reheat soup if refrigerated.) Add vegetables from each group in sequence and cook until longest-cooking vegetables are tender when pierced. Season to taste with salt. Offer sour cream, Parmesan cheese, and lemon wedges to add to taste. Makes 12 to 14 servings.

**Suggested vegetables.** *Thirty minutes' cooking time:* Beets (if used in a large amount, they add red tint to soup and other vegetables), carrots, eggplant, onions, parsley root, parsnips, potatoes, rutabagas, salsify, hard (winter) squash, and turnips.

*Fifteen minutes' cooking time:* Green beans, Oriental long beans, wax beans, bok choy, Brussels sprouts, cauliflower, celery, fennel, Jerusalem artichokes, kohlrabi, okra, bell peppers, mild chiles, and white stems of Swiss chard.

*Five minutes' cooking time:* Italian green beans, broccoli, cabbage, corn (kernels or about 1-inch lengths, including cob), leafy greens, and summer squash.

Tomatoes can be added at any stage to contribute flavor and color.

*Per serving: 232 calories, 21 g protein, 20 g carbohydrates, 8 g total fat, 35 mg cholesterol, 1794 mg sodium*

# Lamb, Dill & Carrot Stew

*Preparation time: 20 minutes*

*Cooking time: About 2 hours*

Braise lamb in red wine with carrots and onions to make this splendid, dill-seasoned stew.

    3   pounds boneless lean lamb stew meat, cut into 1½- to 2-inch cubes
        About 2 cups dry red wine
    ½   cup chopped fresh dill or 1 teaspoon dill weed
    4   small onions (*each* about 2 inches in diameter), cut into quarters
    6   medium-size carrots, cut into 2-inch lengths
    ½   cup whipping cream
        Salt and pepper

In a 5- to 6-quart pan, combine lamb and ½ cup of the wine. Bring to a boil over medium heat; cover and cook for 30 minutes. Uncover and cook until liquid has evaporated; then continue to cook, turning lamb as needed, until browned on all sides (about 30 more minutes). Lift out lamb and set aside. Spoon off and discard any fat.

To pan add dill and 1½ more cups of the wine, stirring to scrape up browned bits. Return lamb to pan and add onions and carrots. Reduce heat to medium-low, cover, and simmer, stirring occasionally, until lamb is very tender when pierced (about 1 hour). If necessary, add more wine to keep liquid ¼ to ½ inch deep.

Add cream and stir just until sauce boils. Season to taste with salt and pepper. Insulate to transport hot (see page 5). Makes 6 to 8 servings.

*Per serving: 333 calories, 33 g protein, 9 g carbohydrates, 18 g total fat, 136 mg cholesterol, 138 mg sodium*

# Veal Spiral Loaf

*Preparation time: 30 minutes*

*Baking time: 1¼ to 1½ hours*

*Chilling time: At least 1 hour*

Meat loaf is back in style. This glorified version, a spiral of ground veal, prosciutto, parsley, and Swiss cheese, makes a grand entrance at any party.

    2   eggs
    2   pounds ground veal
    ¾   cup fresh bread crumbs
    ½   cup tomato juice
    ⅓   cup finely chopped green onions (including tops)
    ¾   teaspoon dry oregano
    ¼   teaspoon *each* salt and pepper
    8   thin slices (2 to 4 oz.) prosciutto or cooked ham
    1½  cups (6 oz.) shredded Swiss cheese
    ½   cup finely chopped parsley
    3   thin slices (about 3 inches square) Swiss cheese, cut in half diagonally
        Parsley Mayonnaise (recipe follows)

In a large bowl, beat eggs until blended. Add veal, bread crumbs, tomato juice, green onions, oregano, salt, and pepper; mix lightly until blended.

On a 12- by 15-inch piece of foil, pat meat mixture into a 9- by 13-inch rectangle. Arrange prosciutto on top, leaving a ½-inch margin on all sides. Sprinkle with shredded cheese and parsley. Starting with a short side, carefully roll up, jelly roll style, using foil to lift meat. Peel off and discard foil. Pinch edges of meat mixture to seal. Place roll, seam side down, in a greased 5- by 9-inch loaf pan.

Bake, uncovered, in a 350° oven until meat is no longer soft in center when a small knife is inserted (1¼ to 1½ hours). Overlap cheese slices on top and continue baking just until cheese is melted (about 2 more minutes). Let cool; then cover and refrigerate for at least 1 hour or for up to a day. Meanwhile, prepare Parsley Mayonnaise. Transport veal loaf (in pan) and mayonnaise separately in a cooler.

To serve, lift out meat and cut into thick slices. Offer mayonnaise to add to taste. Makes 6 to 8 servings.

***Parsley Mayonnaise.*** Mix 1 cup **mayonnaise;** 3 cloves **garlic,** minced or pressed; ⅔ cup finely chopped **parsley;** and 2 teaspoons **dry oregano.** Season to taste with **salt** and **pepper.** If made ahead, cover and refrigerate for up to a day. Makes about 1¼ cups.

*Per serving veal loaf: 346 calories, 33 g protein, 4 g carbohydrates, 21 g total fat, 178 mg cholesterol, 415 mg sodium*

*Per tablespoon mayonnaise: 81 calories, .19 g protein, .65 g carbohydrate, 9 g total fat, 6 mg cholesterol, 63 mg sodium*

**Sweet Indulgence**

*Try one, two, or taste all three. Too tempting to resist are (clockwise from top)
Spiced Applesauce Cupcakes (page 89), Carrot-Zucchini Cake (page 88), and
Chocolate Truffles (page 93).*

# Desserts

When dessert is your potluck assignment, rejoice! Such wonderful choices abound that decision-making will be your only problem. No matter which sweet you choose, expect an enthusiastic reception. Dessert is a universal favorite at potlucks, as elsewhere.

So take your pick from the following pages. Will it be a tender pound cake, a basket of crunchy cookies, or an old-fashioned fruit crisp, still warm from the oven? You'll find our recipes so tempting that you won't want to wait for a potluck to start baking.

## Old-fashioned Pear Spice Cake

Preparation time: 25 minutes

Baking time: 50 to 55 minutes

Perfect for the PTA's holiday gathering, this moist spice cake with cream cheese frosting will disappear as fast as you can serve it.

- 1½ cups *each* sugar and salad oil
- 2 teaspoons *each* baking powder, baking soda, and ground cinnamon
- ½ teaspoon *each* ground ginger and salt
- 2 cups all-purpose flour
- 4 eggs
- 3 medium-size firm-ripe pears (about 1¾ lbs. *total*), peeled, cored, and diced
- ½ cup chopped almonds or walnuts
  Cream Cheese Frosting (recipe follows)

In the large bowl of an electric mixer, combine sugar, oil, baking powder, baking soda, cinnamon, ginger, salt, and flour. Mix to blend; then beat at medium-high speed for 5 minutes. Add eggs, one at a time, beating well after each addition.

Using a rubber spatula, fold pears and nuts into batter. Spread in an ungreased 9- by 13-inch baking pan.

Bake in a 350° oven until a wooden pick inserted in center comes out clean (50 to 55 minutes). Let cool in pan on a wire rack. Meanwhile, prepare Cream Cheese Frosting. Spread frosting over cooled cake. Makes 12 servings.

***Cream Cheese Frosting.*** Combine ¼ cup **butter** or margarine, at room temperature; 1 small package (3 oz.) **cream cheese,** at room temperature; and 1 teaspoon **vanilla.** Beat until fluffy. Gradually beat in 2½ cups sifted **powdered sugar** until frosting is of a good spreading consistency.

*Per serving: 649 calories, 6 g protein, 73 g carbohydrates, 39 g total fat, 109 mg cholesterol, 384 mg sodium*

## Carrot-Zucchini Cake

*Pictured on page 86*

◼◼

*Preparation time: 20 minutes*

*Baking time: About 1 hour*

Carrots and zucchini, along with crushed pine-apple, give this cake special richness of flavor and texture.

> 3 cups all-purpose flour
> 2 cups sugar
> 1½ cups chopped walnuts
> 1½ teaspoons ground cinnamon
> 1 teaspoon *each* baking powder and baking soda
> ½ teaspoon salt
> 2 cans (8 oz. *each*) crushed pineapple
> 1 cup *each* coarsely shredded carrots, coarsely shredded zucchini, and salad oil
> 4 eggs
> 2 teaspoons vanilla
> Pineapple Glaze (recipe follows)

In a large bowl, stir together flour, sugar, walnuts, cinnamon, baking powder, baking soda, and salt. Set aside.

Drain pineapple, reserving juice for glaze. Place pineapple in the large bowl of an electric mixer, along with carrots, zucchini, oil, eggs, and vanilla; beat until well combined. Add to flour mixture, stirring until evenly moistened, and spoon into a well-greased, flour-dusted 10-inch (12-cup) plain or decorative tube pan.

Bake in a 350° oven until a wooden skewer inserted in center comes out clean (about 1 hour). Let cool in pan on a wire rack for 15 minutes.

Then loosen edges and invert onto rack; let stand until cool.

Prepare Pineapple Glaze and drizzle over cake. Makes 12 servings.

**Pineapple Glaze.** Mix 1 cup sifted **powdered sugar** and about 2 tablespoons of the **reserved pineapple juice** until smoothly blended and of a good drizzling consistency.

*Per serving: 589 calories, 8 g protein, 76 g carbohydrates, 30 g total fat, 93 mg cholesterol, 225 mg sodium*

## Sour Cream Pound Cake

*Pictured on page 59*

◼◼

*Preparation time: 20 minutes*

*Baking time: 1¼ to 1½ hours*

A classic dessert, this smooth, fine-textured cake with its fruit garnish looks as delicious as it tastes.

> 6 eggs, separated
> 2½ cups granulated sugar
> 1 cup (½ lb.) butter or margarine, at room temperature
> ½ teaspoon ground mace or nutmeg
> ¼ teaspoon baking soda
> 3 cups sifted cake flour
> 1 cup sour cream
> Powdered sugar
> Seedless grapes, sweet cherries, or strawberries (optional)

In the large bowl of an electric mixer, beat egg whites at high speed until foamy. Gradually beat in ½ cup of the granulated sugar until whites hold soft, moist peaks. Set aside.

In another large bowl, beat butter and remaining 2 cups granulated sugar until creamy. Beat in egg yolks, one at a time, beating well after each addition. Mix in mace and baking soda. Alternately add flour and sour cream, about a third of each at a time, beating until smooth after each addition. Fold in egg whites lightly but thoroughly.

Spoon batter into a well-greased, flour-dusted 10-inch (12- to 14-cup) plain or decorative tube pan.

Bake in a 300° oven until a wooden skewer inserted in center comes out clean (1¼ to 1½ hours). Let cool in pan on a wire rack for 5 minutes. Then loosen edges and invert onto rack; let stand until cool.

Before serving, dust with powdered sugar and, if desired, garnish with fruit. Makes 16 to 18 servings.

*Per serving: 310 calories, 4 g protein, 41 g carbohydrates, 15 g total fat, 125 mg cholesterol, 146 mg sodium*

# Amaretto Cheesecake

*Pictured on page 94 and front cover*

◼

*Preparation time: 15 minutes*

*Baking time: About 1½ hours*

*Cooling and chilling time: About 3 hours*

To present this creamy creation with style, garnish the top with a ring of plump fresh strawberries and a generous sprinkling of toasted sliced almonds.

　　Almond Crust (recipe follows)
1½　pounds cream cheese, at room temperature
1⅓　cups sugar
　4　eggs
　½　teaspoon grated lemon peel
　2　tablespoons lemon juice
　3　tablespoons almond liqueur or 1 teaspoon almond extract
　1　teaspoon vanilla
　½　cup sour cream
　　Strawberries (optional)
　　Toasted sliced almonds (optional)
　　Mint sprigs (optional)

Prepare Almond Crust. Press firmly over bottom of a 10-inch spring-form pan. Bake in a 325° oven until crust begins to brown and feels firm (10 to 12 minutes). Set aside on a rack.

　　In the large bowl of an electric mixer, beat cream cheese and sugar until fluffy. Add eggs, lemon peel, lemon juice, liqueur, vanilla, and sour cream; beat until well combined. Pour over crust.

　　Bake in a 325° oven until top is golden and center is set when gently shaken (about 1¼ hours). Let cool in pan on a rack; then cover and refrigerate for at least 2 hours or for up to a day. Transport in a cooler.

　　Before serving, remove pan sides and garnish, if desired, with strawberries, almonds, and mint sprigs. Makes 10 to 12 servings.

***Almond Crust.*** In a food processor or blender, whirl about 2 cups crisp **almond macaroons** to make ¾ cup crumbs; transfer crumbs to a bowl.

Whirl ½ cup **almonds** until powdery. Add to crumbs and mix with 3 tablespoons melted **butter** or margarine until well combined.

*Per serving: 457 calories, 8 g protein, 36 g carbohydrates, 31 g total fat, 171 mg cholesterol, 258 mg sodium*

# Spiced Applesauce Cupcakes

*Pictured on page 86*

◼

*Preparation time: 15 minutes*

*Baking time: 20 to 25 minutes*

From a practical point of view, these cupcakes are easily portable, and they're ideal for a serve-your-self buffet. Sugar-glazed and crunchy with pecans, they're also incredibly good to eat.

1¾　cups all-purpose flour
　1　teaspoon *each* baking soda, ground cinnamon, and ground nutmeg
　¼　teaspoon ground cloves
　½　teaspoon salt
　½　cup (¼ lb.) butter or margarine, at room temperature
　1　cup sugar
　1　egg
　1　cup unsweetened canned applesauce
　1　cup finely chopped pecans
　　Apple Glaze (recipe follows)

Stir together flour, baking soda, cinnamon, nutmeg, cloves, and salt until very well combined. Set aside.

　　In the large bowl of an electric mixer, beat butter and sugar until creamy; add egg and beat until fluffy. Stir in applesauce. Gradually add flour mixture, beating until well blended. Stir in nuts. Spoon batter into paper-lined or well-greased 2½-inch muffin pans, filling each about two-thirds full.

　　Bake in a 350° oven until tops spring back when lightly touched (20 to 25 minutes). Let cool in pans on wire racks for about 5 minutes. Prepare Apple Glaze. Carefully remove cupcakes, place on racks, and brush with glaze. Makes 1½ dozen cupcakes.

***Apple Glaze.*** Mix ¾ cup sifted **powdered sugar** and about 5 teaspoons **apple juice** or orange juice until smoothly blended and of a good brushing consistency.

*Per cupcake: 200 calories, 2 g protein, 27 g carbohydrates, 10 g total fat, 29 mg cholesterol, 163 mg sodium*

## Giant Walnut Crumb Cooky

*Pictured on facing page*

■■
■

*Preparation time: 10 minutes*

*Baking time: 35 to 40 minutes*

One giant, crumbly cooky can put broad smiles on guests' faces as they break off chunks to nibble.

- 1 cup walnuts
- 2½ cups all-purpose flour
- 1 cup granulated sugar
- 1 cup (½ lb.) cold butter or margarine
  Powdered sugar (optional)

In a food processor or blender, whirl nuts until finely ground. Mix nuts, flour, and granulated sugar. With food processor or a pastry blender, cut in butter until mixture forms fine, even crumbs (mixture should remain crumbly). Spread in a greased, flour-dusted 12-inch pizza pan; do not press down. Bake in a 350° oven until lightly browned (35 to 40 minutes). Let cool in pan on a wire rack.

Slide cooky from pan onto rack. Sprinkle lightly with powdered sugar, if desired. If made ahead, store airtight for up to a day. Break into chunks to eat. Makes 12 to 18 servings.

*Per serving: 239 calories, 3 g protein, 25 g carbohydrates, 15 g total fat, 28 mg cholesterol, 105 mg sodium*

## Oat-Nut Chocolate Chip Crisps

*Pictured on facing page*

■■
■

*Preparation time: 15 minutes*

*Baking time: 12 to 14 minutes*

Cooky connoisseurs of all ages are sure to love this combination of classic cooky ingredients.

- 1 teaspoon baking soda
- 1 cup all-purpose flour
- 1 cup (½ lb.) butter or margarine, at room temperature
- ¾ cup firmly packed brown sugar
- ½ cup granulated sugar
- 2 eggs
- 1 teaspoon vanilla
- 2 cups rolled oats

- 1 cup finely chopped walnuts or pecans
- 1 cup miniature semisweet chocolate chips

Stir together baking soda and flour until well combined. Set aside.

In the large bowl of an electric mixer, beat butter, brown sugar, and granulated sugar until creamy. Beat in eggs, one at a time. Mix in vanilla. Gradually add flour mixture, beating until well blended. Stir in oats, nuts, and chocolate chips.

For each cooky, drop a rounded tablespoon of dough on a greased baking sheet, spacing cookies about 2 inches apart. Bake in a 375° oven until golden (12 to 14 minutes). Let cool on baking sheet on a wire rack for about 2 minutes; then transfer cookies to racks to cool completely. If made ahead, store airtight for up to 2 days or freeze for longer storage. Makes about 4½ dozen cookies.

*Per cooky: 102 calories, 1 g protein, 11 g carbohydrates, 6 g total fat, 19 mg cholesterol, 54 mg sodium*

## Dark Chocolate Chewy Brownies

*Pictured on facing page*

■■
■

*Preparation time: 15 minutes*

*Baking time: 25 to 30 minutes*

Deliver rich and chewy chocolate extravagance with a plateful of luscious brownies.

- 1 cup (½ lb.) butter or margarine, cut into chunks
- 6 ounces unsweetened chocolate
- 2⅔ cups sugar
- 4 eggs
- 2 teaspoons vanilla
- 1 cup all-purpose flour
- 1 cup slivered almonds or chopped walnuts

Combine butter and chocolate in a 3- to 4-quart pan and place over low heat. When ingredients begin to soften, stir until blended; remove from heat. Add sugar, eggs, and vanilla; beat with an electric mixer until smooth. Blend in flour. Spread in a greased 9-by 13-inch baking pan; sprinkle with nuts.

Bake in a 350° oven just until edges feel firm and center springs back when gently pressed (25 to 30 minutes). Let cool in pan on a wire rack. Cut into bars. Makes 12 to 18 servings.

*Per serving: 341 calories, 5 g protein, 39 g carbohydrates, 20 g total fat, 88 mg cholesterol, 121 mg sodium*

**For the Milk & Cooky Crowd**

*Nothing delights kids—of any age—quite like freshly baked cookies with cold milk.
Enjoy (clockwise from top) Giant Walnut Crumb Cooky, Oat-Nut Chocolate Chip
Crisps, and Dark Chocolate Chewy Brownies (recipes on facing page).*

# Fruit Crisp

*Pictured on page 35*

*Preparation time: About 30 minutes*

*Baking time: About 50 minutes*

A buttery topping of oatmeal and brown sugar seals in the juices of this traditional baked dessert. Let it showcase fresh peaches, pears, or apples.

| | |
|---|---|
| 8 | cups (about 4 lbs.) thinly sliced peeled peaches, pears, or apples |
| ¼ | cup lemon juice |
| 1 | cup sugar |
| ½ | teaspoon ground cinnamon |
| ½ | cup water |
| | Oatmeal Topping (recipe follows) |

In a 9- by 13-inch baking dish, mix fruit, lemon juice, sugar, and cinnamon. Pour water over mixture.

Prepare Oatmeal Topping. Crumble evenly over fruit mixture. Bake in a 375° oven until top is golden brown and fruit is tender (about 50 minutes). Makes 10 to 12 servings.

**Oatmeal Topping.** Stir together 1½ cups *each* **all-purpose flour** and firmly packed **brown sugar,** 2½ cups **rolled oats,** ¼ cup **nonfat dry milk,** 1½ teaspoons **ground cinnamon,** and ½ teaspoon **ground ginger.** Cut in 1 cup (½ lb.) firm **butter** or margarine until mixture forms large crumbs.

*Per serving: 496 calories, 6 g protein, 84 g carbohydrates, 17 g total fat, 42 mg cholesterol, 174 mg sodium*

# Glazed Berry Tarts

*Pictured on page 30*

*Preparation time: 35 minutes*

*Baking time: About 20 minutes*

One rich bite of this tiny berry-crowned tart goes a long way. Two, and the tart disappears altogether. Choose raspberries, blackberries, or boysenberries.

| | |
|---|---|
| 1 | cup all-purpose flour |
| 2 | tablespoons granulated sugar |
| 6 | tablespoons cold butter or margarine |
| 1 | egg yolk |
| 2 | packages (3 oz. *each*) cream cheese, at room temperature |
| 2 | tablespoons powdered sugar |
| ½ | teaspoon grated lemon peel |
| 1 | tablespoon kirsch or lemon juice |
| 2½ | cups raspberries, blackberries, or boysenberries |
| ⅓ | cup currant jelly |

In a bowl or food processor, stir together flour and granulated sugar. Add butter and rub with your fingers (or whirl in processor) until fine crumbs form. With a fork (or whirling in processor), stir in egg yolk until dough holds together.

For each tart, press a rounded tablespoon of the pastry over bottom and sides of a 2-inch muffin pan or 2½-inch tart pan. Bake in a 300° oven until golden (about 20 minutes). Let cool in pans on a wire rack; then ease out carefully and place on rack.

Beat cream cheese and powdered sugar until creamy. Beat in lemon peel and kirsch. Spoon about 1 tablespoon of the mixture into each tart shell. Top with berries, dividing fruit evenly.

In a small pan, melt jelly over low heat. Brush over berries. If made ahead, cover and refrigerate for up to a day. Transport in a cooler. Makes 1 dozen tarts.

*Per tart: 195 calories, 3 g protein, 21 g carbohydrates, 11 g total fat, 54 mg cholesterol, 103 mg sodium*

# Almond Toffee Tart

*Pictured on page 78*

*Preparation time: About 20 minutes*

*Baking time: 45 to 50 minutes*

Thin, rich, and studded with nuts, this golden toffee tart brings any potluck dinner to a delicious conclusion. If you wish, you can substitute hazelnuts for the almonds in the filling.

| | |
|---|---|
| | Press-in Pastry (recipe follows) |
| 1½ | cups *each* whipping cream and sugar |
| ½ | teaspoon grated orange peel |
| ¼ | teaspoon salt |
| 2 | cups (about 6 oz.) sliced almonds or coarsely chopped hazelnuts (filberts) |
| ¼ | teaspoon almond extract |

Prepare Press-in Pastry and set aside.

In a 2- to 3-quart pan, combine cream, sugar, orange peel, and salt. Bring to a boil over high heat, stirring occasionally. Reduce heat to medium and cook, stirring often, for 5 minutes. Remove from heat and stir in nuts and almond extract. Spread nut mixture in pastry shell.

Bake in a 375° oven until lightly browned (about 35 minutes for a 12-inch tart, 40 minutes for an 11-inch tart). Let cool in pan on a wire rack until just warm to touch. Remove pan sides. If made ahead, cover lightly and let stand at room temperature for up to a day.

To serve, cut into thin wedges. Makes 10 to 12 servings.

***Press-in Pastry.*** In a bowl or food processor, stir together 2 cups **all-purpose flour** and 3 tablespoons **sugar**. Add ¾ cup (⅜ lb.) cold **butter** or margarine, cut into chunks, and rub with your fingers (or whirl in processor) until fine crumbs form. With a fork (or whirling in processor), stir in 2 **egg yolks** until dough holds together.

Press dough evenly over bottom and sides of an 11- or 12-inch tart pan with a removable bottom. Bake in a 325° oven until pale gold (10 to 12 minutes).

*Per serving: 467 calories, 6 g protein, 48 g carbohydrates, 29 g total fat, 110 mg cholesterol, 176 mg sodium*

# Chocolate Chip Pie

Preparation time: 25 minutes

Baking time: 50 to 60 minutes

This chocolate-flecked dessert will delight the taste buds on its own merit alone. But to really show it off, top it with whipped cream or ice cream.

    Flaky Pastry (recipe follows)
2  eggs
½  cup (¼ lb.) butter or margarine, melted and cooled
1  cup sugar
1  teaspoon vanilla
2  tablespoons bourbon or water
¾  cup all-purpose flour
1  cup chopped pecans or walnuts
1  package (6 oz.) semisweet chocolate chips
    Whipped cream or ice cream (optional)

Prepare Flaky Pastry. On a lightly floured board, roll out pastry into an 11-inch circle and fit into a 9-inch pie pan; trim and flute edge. Set aside.

In the large bowl of an electric mixer, beat eggs, butter, sugar, vanilla, and bourbon until well blended. Stir in flour, pecans, and chocolate chips. Spread batter in pastry shell. Bake in a 350° oven until a wooden pick inserted in center comes out clean (50 to 60 minutes).

Before serving, garnish with whipped cream, if desired. Makes 8 servings.

***Flaky Pastry.*** Stir together 1 cup **all-purpose flour** and ⅛ teaspoon **salt**. Using a pastry blender or 2 knives, cut in ⅓ cup **solid vegetable shortening** until mixture resembles coarse meal. Stirring lightly and quickly with a fork, gradually sprinkle 2 to 3 tablespoons **cold water,** a tablespoon at a time, over mixture, stirring just until all flour is moistened and dough begins to cling together. With your hands, gather dough into a ball.

*Per serving: 600 calories, 6 g protein, 61 g carbohydrates, 38 g total fat, 100 mg cholesterol, 170 mg sodium*

# Chocolate Truffles

Pictured on page 86

Preparation time: 30 minutes

Chilling time: 40 to 45 minutes

The ultimate experience for chocolate fanciers, these meltingly rich and creamy sweets are very easy to make. Offer them with coffee and liqueurs or brandy to bring a potluck dinner to an elegant ending.

8  ounces semisweet chocolate, coarsely chopped
¼  cup whipping cream
3  tablespoons ground sweet chocolate or cocoa

Place semisweet chocolate and cream in a 1½- to 2-quart pan over lowest possible heat. Stir often until chocolate is melted and mixture is well blended. Transfer to a bowl; cover and refrigerate just until mixture is firm enough to hold its shape (40 to 45 minutes). Meanwhile, spread ground chocolate in a shallow pan or on wax paper.

Using your fingers or 2 spoons, quickly shape about 1 teaspoon of the chocolate mixture at a time into a ball and roll in ground chocolate until coated. If desired, place truffles in small paper bonbon cups. If made ahead, cover and refrigerate for up to 2 weeks. Makes about 2 dozen truffles.

*Per truffle: 59 calories, .49 g protein, 6 g carbohydrates, 4 g total fat, 3 mg cholesterol, 2 mg sodium*

**Grand Finale**

*Lusciously decked out with strawberries and almonds, Amaretto Cheesecake
(page 89) makes a tantalizing dessert. On the same potluck menu are Baked Fish
with Mushroom Sauce (page 52), top left, and Tarragon-marinated Vegetable
Platter (page 25), top right.*

# Index

**A**

Almond
 crust, 89
 tart, fresh apricot-, 10
 toffee tart, 92
Amaretto cheesecake, 89
Anchovy
 dressing, 45
 sauce, eggplant, olive &, 13
Appetizers
 artichoke hearts with blue cheese, 20
 Belgian endive & smoked salmon appetizer, 15
 bell peppers with peppercorn dip, 16
 chile-cheese spread, 17
 chili chicken chunks, 18
 cranberry cocktail meatballs, 21
 dried tomato torta, 17
 garden-fresh bagna cauda, 16
 melted Brie in crust, 20
 pistachio-turkey appetizer cups, 21
 quick chicken liver pâté, 18
 shrimp on palm pedestals, 60
 vegetable-cheese nachos, 16
Apple
 brunch cake, spiced, 8
 cider stew, 73
 glaze, 89
Applesauce cupcakes, spiced, 89
Apricot-almond tart, fresh, 10
Artichoke hearts with blue cheese, 20
Artichokes, tiny lemon-scented, 9
Avocado
 pinwheels, turkey & mint-, 68
 sauce, creamy, 48

**B**

Bagna cauda, garden-fresh, 16
Baked beans, sweet & sour, 37
Baked chicken legs, Mexican-style, 64
Baked fish with horseradish cream sauce, 52
Baked fish with mushroom sauce, 52
Basil
 dressing, 24
 & scallop pasta salad, 45
Bean(s)
 baked, sweet & sour, 37
 cassoulet, black, 79
 green, Oriental, 36
 & ham salad, crunchy rice, 81
 slow-cooked ribs &, 79
 white, & cherry tomato salad, 26
Beef
 apple cider stew, 73
 casserole, three-layer, 71
 cranberry cocktail meatballs, 21
 cubes, wine-simmered, 73
 harvest soup, 84
 Hungarian cabbage rolls, 72
 machaca burritos, 74
 open-faced tamale pie, 72
 oven-simmered chile short ribs, 74
 sausage meat loaf, 77
 spicy Mediterranean meatballs, 12
Belgian endive & smoked salmon appetizer, 15
Bell peppers with peppercorn dip, 16
Berry tarts, glazed, 92
Black bean cassoulet, 79
Blue cheese, artichoke hearts with, 20
Breads
 herb, 29
 old-fashioned lemon, 8
 Parmesan cheese, 29
 whole wheat country loaf, 29
Brie, melted, in crust, 20
Broccoli
 Milanese, 61
 & mushrooms, marinated, 26

Brownies, dark chocolate chewy, 90
Bulgur
 & rice pilaf, 41
 salad, crunchy vegetable &, 32
Burritos, machaca, 74

**C**

Cabbage rolls, Hungarian, 72
Cakes
 carrot-zucchini, 88
 cranberry brunch, 8
 old-fashioned pear spice, 87
 sour cream pound, 88
 spiced apple brunch, 8
 *See also* Cheesecakes; Tarts
Cannelloni, eggroll, 63
Carrot
 stew, lamb, dill &, 85
 -zucchini cake, 88
Casseroles
 chicken, chile & cheese, 65
 clam & noodle, 53
 green onion–rice, 41
 high desert corn, 33
 layered enchilada, 37
 layered spinach, 40
 mostaccioli & Swiss cheese, 81
 potato-cheese, 40
 red snapper, 49
 three-layer beef, 71
 zucchini jack, 40
Cassoulet, black bean, 79
Cauliflower & zucchini with tahini, 24
Chard, feta & fila pie, 39
Cheesecakes
 amaretto, 89
 pumpkin, 61
Cheese(s)
 blue, artichoke hearts with, 20
 bread, Parmesan, 29
 casserole, chicken, chile &, 65
 casserole, potato-, 40
 chard, feta & fila pie, 39
 melted Brie in crust, 20
 nachos, vegetable-, 16
 spread, chili-, 17
 Swiss, casserole, mostaccioli &, 81
 Swiss mushroom spaghetti squash, 34
 turnover, Italian meat &, 82
 two, pork loin stuffed with, 9
 zucchini jack casserole, 40
Cherry tomato
 salad, white bean &, 26
 topping, 65
Chicken
 black bean cassoulet, 79
 chile & cheese casserole, 65
 chili sauce, 12
 chunks, chili, 18
 crispy oven-fried, for a dozen, 64
 eggroll cannelloni, 63
 Florentine, 63
 legs, baked, Mexican-style, 64
 liver pâté, quick, 18
 Parmesan Dijon, 63
 -prosciutto filling, 63
 rice & tomatillo bake, 64
 salad, curry & fruit, 55
 salad, overnight layered, 57
 salad, sourdough chili, 57
 -spinach salad with cilantro, 56
 stew, Cuban, 58
 Waldorf salad, mustard, 56
Chile
 & cheese casserole, chicken, 65
 crêpes, turkey &, 68
 short ribs, oven-simmered, 74
 shrimp & corn salad, 47
Chili
 -cheese, spread, 17
 chicken chunks, 18
 chicken salad, sourdough, 57
 dressing, 57
 Oregonian turkey, 69
 sauce, chicken, 12
Chocolate
 dark, chewy brownies, 90
 truffles, 93
Chocolate chip
 crisps, oat-nut, 90
 pie, 93

Chowder, seafood, for a crowd, 49
Cider
 hot buttered, 8
 stew, apple, 73
Cilantro
 chicken-spinach salad with, 56
 dressing, 56
Clam & noodle casserole, 53
Cold food, transporting, 5
Cookies
 giant walnut crumb, 90
 oat-nut chocolate chip crisps, 90
Cool poached fish with sauce, 48
Cool salmon steaks & vegetables, 47
Corn
 casserole, high desert, 33
 coblets, sweet, 33
 salad, chile shrimp &, 47
Cornmeal crust, 72
Cranberry
 brunch cake, 8
 cocktail meatballs, 21
 -port relish, 61
Cream cheese frosting, 87
Creamy sausage & mushroom sauce, 13
Crêpe(s), 50
 shrimp stack, 50
 tender, 69
 turkey & chile, 68
Crispy oven-fried chicken for a dozen, 64
Crunchy rice, bean & ham salad, 81
Crunchy vegetable & bulgur salad, 32
Crunchy vegetable sauce, 13
Cuban chicken stew, 58
Cumin rice with peas, 74
Cupcakes, spiced applesauce, 89
Curried ham & rice rolls, 7
Curry & fruit chicken salad, 55

**D**

Dark chocolate chewy brownies, 90
Desserts
 almond toffee tart, 92
 amaretto cheesecake, 89
 carrot-zucchini cake, 88
 chocolate chip pie, 93
 chocolate truffles, 93
 cranberry brunch cake, 8
 dark chocolate chewy brownies, 90
 fresh apricot-almond tart, 10
 fruit crisp, 92
 giant walnut crumb cooky, 90
 glazed berry tarts, 92
 oat-nut chocolate chip crisps, 90
 old-fashioned pear spice cake, 87
 pumpkin cheesecake, 61
 raspberry jam tart, 10
 sour cream pound cake, 88
 spiced applesauce cupcakes, 89
Dill
 & carrot stew, lamb, 85
 -curry dressing, 55
Dip, peppercorn, bell peppers with, 16
Dried tomato torta, 17

**E**

Eggplant
 Monterey, 34
 olive & anchovy sauce, 13
 oven-browned, 66
 Parmesan, turkey, 66
Eggroll cannelloni, 63
Enchilada casserole, layered, 37
Endive, Belgian, & smoked salmon appetizer, 15

**F**

Feta & fila pie, chard, 39
Fila pie, chard, feta &, 39
Fish
 baked, with horseradish cream sauce, 52
 baked, with mushroom sauce, 52
 cool poached, with sauce, 48
 cool salmon steaks & vegetables, 47
 gravlax plus, 48
 layered Niçoise salad, 45

Fish *(cont'd.)*
 oven-poached, 52
 red snapper casserole, 49
 salad, Veracruz, 42
 sashimi tray salad, 44
 seafood chowder for a crowd, 49
 sole fillets with four-color vegetable salad, 44
 tuna & spaghetti bake, 50
Flaky pastry, 93
Fresh apricot-almond tart, 10
Frittata, zucchini, 7
Fruit
 chicken salad, curry &, 55
 crisp, 92

**G**

Garden-fresh bagna cauda, 16
Garlic cream dressing, green salad with, 77
Giant walnut crumb cooky, 90
Glazed berry tarts, 92
Graham cracker crust, 61
Gravlax plus, 48
Greek peasant salad, 23
Green beans Oriental, 36
Green onion–rice casserole, 41
Green salad
 with garlic cream dressing, 77
 overnight layered, 24
Ground beef
 cranberry cocktail meatballs, 21
 Hungarian cabbage rolls, 72
 open-faced tamale pie, 72
 sausage meat loaf, 77
 spicy Mediterranean meatballs, 12
 three-layer beef casserole, 71
Guacamole, 18
Guacamole pasta salad, 32

**H**

Ham
 harvest soup, 84
 Italian meat & cheese turnover, 82
 & rice rolls, curried, 7
 salad, crunchy rice, bean &, 81
Harvest soup party, 84
Herb
 bread, 29
 mayonnaise, steamed turkey breast with, 68
High desert corn casserole, 33
Holiday cheer, 6–8
Holiday turkey dinner, 60–61
Horseradish cream sauce, baked fish with, 52
Hot buttered cider, 8
Hot food, transporting, 5
Hungarian cabbage rolls, 72

**I**

Insulating hot food, 5
Italian meat & cheese turnover, 82

**J**

Jack casserole, zucchini, 40
Jam tart, raspberry, 10

**L**

Lamb
 dill & carrot stew, 85
 & mint filling, 82
Lasagne
 potluck, 76
 scallop, 53
Layered enchilada casserole, 37
Layered Niçoise salad, 45
Layered spinach casserole, 40
Lemon
 -basil dressing, 32
 bread, old-fashioned, 8
 dressing, 23
 -garlic mayonnaise, 24
 -scented artichokes, tiny, 9
Liver pâté, quick chicken, 18

**M**

Machaca burritos, 74
Marinated broccoli & mushrooms, 26
Mayonnaise
 fresh, 56
 herb, steamed turkey breast with, 68

Mayonnaise (cont'd.)
    lemon-garlic, 24
    parsley, 85
Meat & cheese turnover, Italian, 82
Meatballs
    cranberry cocktail, 21
    spicy Mediterranean, 12
Melon balls & pineapple chunks, minted, 7
Melted Brie in crust, 20
Menus
    holiday cheer, 6–8
    holiday turkey dinner, 60–61
    pasta party, 12–13
    spring picnic potluck, 9–11
Mint
    -avocado pinwheels, turkey &, 68
    -avocado spread, 68
Minted melon balls & pineapple chunks, 7
Mixed rice salad, 32
Molded moussaka, 82
Mostaccioli & Swiss cheese casserole, 81
Moussaka, molded, 82
Mushroom(s)
    marinated broccoli &, 26
    sauce, baked fish with, 52
    sauce, creamy sausage &, 13
    spaghetti squash, Swiss, 34
Mustard
    -chicken Waldorf salad, 56
    -dressed pea salad, 28
    sauce, 48

N
Nachos, vegetable-cheese, 16
Niçoise salad, layered, 45
Noodle casserole, clam &, 53
Nut chocolate chip crisps, oat-, 90
Nutritional data, 5

O
Oatmeal topping, 92
Oat-nut chocolate chip crisps, 90
Old-fashioned lemon bread, 8
Old-fashioned pear spice cake, 87
Olive & anchovy sauce, eggplant, 13
Onion
    cream dressing, 28
    green, –rice casserole, 41
    sweet, potato salad, 31
Open-faced tamale pie, 72
Orange, fresh candied, sweet potatoes with, 60
Oregonian turkey chili, 69
Oven-poached fish, 52
Oven-simmered chile short ribs, 74
Overnight layered chicken salad, 57
Overnight layered green salad, 24

P
Palm pedestals, shrimp on, 60
Parmesan, turkey eggplant, 66
Parmesan cheese bread, 29
Parmesan Dijon chicken, 63
Parsley
    mayonnaise, 85
    potato salad, 28
Pasta
    clam & noodle casserole, 53
    mostaccioli & Swiss cheese casserole, 81
    party, 12–13
    potluck lasagne, 76
    salad, basil & scallop, 45
    salad, guacamole, 32
    scallop lasagne, 53
    tuna & spaghetti bake, 50
Pâté, quick chicken liver, 18
Pea
    & roasted pecan slaw, 28
    salad, mustard-dressed, 28
Pear(s)
    pickled strawberries &, 9
    spice cake, old-fashioned, 87
Pecan, roasted, slaw, pea &, 28
Peppercorn dip, bell peppers with, 16
Peppers, bell, with peppercorn dip, 16
Picadillo, pork, 80

Pickled strawberries & pears, 9
Picnic potluck, spring, 9–11
Pies
    chard, feta & fila, 39
    chocolate chip, 93
    open-faced tamale, 72
Pilaf, bulgur & rice, 41
Pineapple
    chunks, minted melon balls &, 7
    glaze, 88
Pistachio-turkey appetizer cups, 21
Planning, potluck, 4–5
Pocket bread toast triangles, 17
Pork
    black bean cassoulet, 79
    chops & potatoes au gratin, 80
    loin stuffed with two cheeses, 9
    picadillo, 80
    sauce, tomato, 76
    sausage meat loaf, 77
    slow-cooked ribs & beans, 79
Port relish, cranberry-, 61
Potato(es)
    -cheese casserole, 40
    au gratin, pork chops &, 80
    Romanoff, 60
    salad, parsley, 28
    salad, sweet onion, 31
    sweet, with fresh candied orange, 60
    & vegetable salad, 31
Potluck lasagne, 76
Potluck planning, 4–5
Poultry. See Chicken; Turkey
Pound cake, sour cream, 88
Press-in pastry, 93
Pumpkin cheesecake, 61

Q
Quick chicken liver pâté, 18

R
Radish tartar sauce, 47
Raspberry jam tart, 10
Red snapper casserole, 49
Relishes
    cranberry-port, 61
    pickled strawberries & pears, 9
Ribs
    & beans, slow-cooked, 79
    short, oven-simmered chile, 74
Rice
    bean & ham salad, crunchy, 81
    casserole, green onion–, 41
    cumin, with peas, 74
    pilaf, bulgur &, 41
    rolls, curried ham &, 7
    salad, mixed, 32
    salad, wild, 10
    & tomatillo bake, chicken, 64

S
Safety, potluck food, 5
Salads
    basil & scallop pasta, 45
    chicken-spinach, with cilantro, 56
    chile shrimp & corn, 47
    crunchy rice, bean & ham, 81
    crunchy vegetable & bulgur, 32
    curry & fruit chicken, 55
    four-color vegetable, sole fillets with, 44
    Greek peasant, 23
    green, with garlic cream dressing, 77
    guacamole pasta, 32
    layered Niçoise, 45
    mixed rice, 32
    mustard-chicken Waldorf, 56
    mustard-dressed pea, 28
    overnight layered chicken, 57
    overnight layered green, 24
    parsley potato, 28
    pea & roasted pecan slaw, 28
    potato & vegetable, 31
    sashimi tray, 44
    sourdough chili chicken, 57
    spinach, with basil dressing, 24
    sweet onion potato, 31
    Veracruz fish, 42
    white bean & cherry tomato, 26
    wild rice, 10

Salmon
    gravlax plus, 48
    smoked, appetizer, Belgian endive &, 15
    steaks & vegetables, cool, 47
Sashimi tray salad, 44
Sauces
    chicken chili, 12
    creamy avocado, 48
    creamy sausage & mushroom, 13
    creamy tomato-mint, 63
    crunchy vegetable, 13
    eggplant, olive & anchovy, 13
    mustard, 48
    radish tartar, 47
    spicy Mediterranean meatballs, 12
    tahini, 25
    tomato pork, 76
Sausage
    black bean cassoulet, 79
    meat loaf, 77
    & mushroom sauce, creamy, 13
Scallop
    lasagne, 53
    pasta salad, basil &, 45
Seafood chowder for a crowd, 49
Shellfish
    basil & scallop pasta salad, 45
    chile shrimp & corn salad, 47
    clam & noodle casserole, 53
    crêpe shrimp stack, 50
    scallop lasagne, 53
    seafood chowder for a crowd, 49
    shrimp on palm pedestals, 60
Short ribs, oven-simmered chile, 74
Shrimp
    & corn salad, chile, 47
    on palm pedestals, 60
    stack, crêpe, 50
Slaw, pea & roasted pecan, 28
Slow-cooked ribs & beans, 79
Smoked salmon appetizer, Belgian endive &, 15
Sole fillets with four-color vegetable salad, 44
Soup, harvest, 84
Sour cream pound cake, 88
Sourdough chili chicken salad, 57
Soy-sesame dressing, 44
Spaghetti bake, tuna &, 50
Spaghetti squash, Swiss mushroom, 34
Spice cake, old-fashioned pear, 87
Spiced apple brunch cake, 8
Spiced applesauce cupcakes, 89
Spicy Mediterranean meatballs, 12
Spinach
    casserole, layered, 40
    salad, chicken-, with cilantro, 56
    salad with basil dressing, 24
Spring picnic potluck, 9–11
Squash
    spaghetti, Swiss mushroom, 34
    summer, gratin, 36
Steamed turkey breast with herb mayonnaise, 68
Stews
    apple cider, 73
    Cuban chicken, 58
    lamb, dill & carrot, 85
Strawberries & pears, pickled, 9
Summer squash gratin, 36
Sweet & sour baked beans, 37
Sweet corn coblets, 33
Sweet onion potato salad, 31
Sweet potatoes with fresh candied orange, 60
Sweet-sour dressing, 81
Swiss cheese casserole, mostaccioli &, 81
Swiss mushroom spaghetti squash, 34
Szechwan peppercorn dressing, 44

T
Tahini
    cauliflower & zucchini with, 24
    sauce, 25
Tamale pie, open-faced, 72
Tarragon
    dressing, 25
    -marinated vegetable platter, 25

Tarts
    almond toffee, 92
    fresh apricot-almond, 10
    glazed berry, 92
    raspberry jam, 10
Three-color vegetable tetrazzini, 39
Three-layer beef casserole, 71
Tiny lemon-scented artichokes, 9
Toffee tart, almond, 92
Tomatillo bake, chicken, rice &, 64
Tomato
    cherry, salad, white bean &, 26
    -mint sauce, creamy, 63
    pork sauce, 76
    torta, dried, 17
Torta, dried tomato, 17
Transporting food, 5
Truffles, chocolate, 93
Tuna
    layered Niçoise salad, 45
    & spaghetti bake, 50
    turkey tonnato, 66
Turkey
    appetizer cups, pistachio-, 21
    breast, steamed, with herb mayonnaise, 68
    & chile crêpes, 69
    chili, Oregonian, 69
    dinner, holiday, 60–61
    eggplant Parmesan, 66
    Italian meat & cheese turnover, 82
    & mint-avocado pinwheels, 68
    tonnato, 66

V
Veal spiral loaf, 85
Vegetable(s)
    broccoli Milanese, 61
    cauliflower & zucchini with tahini, 24
    chard, feta & fila pie, 39
    -cheese nachos, 16
    cool salmon steaks &, 47
    crunchy, & bulgur salad, 32
    eggplant Monterey, 34
    garden-fresh, 16
    green beans Oriental, 36
    green onion–rice casserole, 41
    harvest soup, 84
    high desert corn casserole, 33
    layered enchilada casserole, 37
    layered spinach casserole, 40
    marinated broccoli & mushrooms, 26
    platter, tarragon-marinated, 25
    potato-cheese casserole, 40
    potatoes Romanoff, 60
    salad, four-color, sole fillets with, 44
    salad, potato &, 31
    sauce, crunchy, 13
    summer squash gratin, 36
    sweet corn coblets, 33
    sweet potatoes with fresh candied orange, 60
    sweet & sour baked beans, 37
    Swiss mushroom spaghetti squash, 34
    tetrazzini, three-color, 39
    three-color vegetable tetrazzini, 39
    tiny lemon-scented artichokes, 9
    zucchini jack casserole, 40
Veracruz fish salad, 42

W
Waldorf salad, mustard-chicken, 56
Walnut crumb cooky, giant, 90
White bean & cherry tomato salad, 26
Whole wheat country loaf, 29
Wild rice salad, 10
Wine-simmered beef cubes, 73

Y
Yogurt dressing, 31

Z
Zucchini
    cake, carrot-, 88
    cauliflower &, with tahini, 24
    frittata, 7
    jack casserole, 40